How
Not
to
Screw
It
Up

ALSO BY NITA TUCKER

How Not to Stay Single:
10 Steps to a Great Relationship

How *Not* to Screw It Up

10 *Steps*
to an Extraordinary
Relationship

NITA TUCKER

Three Rivers Press / NEW YORK

Published by Three Rivers Press, a division of Crown Publishers, Inc.,
201 East 50th Street, New York, New York 10022. Member of the
Crown Publishing Group.

Random House, Inc. New York, Toronto, London, Sydney, Auckland
www.randomhouse.com

Three Rivers Press is a trademark of Crown Publishers, Inc.

Printed in the United States of America

Design by Cathryn S. Aison

Library of Congress Cataloging-in-Publication Data
Tucker, Nita.
How not to screw it up: 10 steps to an extraordinary relationship /
by Nita Tucker.
1. Marriage.   2. Man-woman relationships.   I. Title.
HQ734.T89   1999
646.7'8—dc21   98-21370
CIP

ISBN: 0-609-80333-6

BVG 01

In loving memory of my parents,
Ann and Louis Fisher

My special thanks go to:

Terry and Alan Axelrod, Sylvia and Zollie Volchok and Abra
    and Howard Edelman—for being the perfect mentors
    in having a lasting, extraordinary relationship.
Harvey Klinger, my agent—for taking me on and believing
    in me.
Shaye Areheart—for being my editor and biggest fan.
Debra Feinstein—for her love, friendship, and generous
    contributions to my work.
Ann Overton—for bringing clarity and power to my words
    on the page.
Geraldine Newman—for her brilliant titles.
Jordan and Montana, my children—who love that their
    parents are wild about each other.
And always to my husband and the love of my life, Tony. My
    love for you is the inspiration for this book—our mar-
    riage is so great, I wanted to make sure I'd never screw
    it up.

Contents

How
Not
to
Screw
It
Up

Introduction

Most people don't get married with the idea that there's a pretty good chance their marriage will not last. But in fact, 75 percent of first marriages and 60 percent of marriages overall are ending in divorce, which means more couples are divorcing than staying together. Yet couple after couple walk down the aisle believing their marriage is different, or this marriage is different from their previous one(s), and therefore it will last. And what are they doing to ensure that they will not be another statistic of failure? Nothing.

We've been taught and conditioned to think that there is nothing to do after the "I do." This book, however, is about some things you can do—not only to prevent divorce but to have an extraordinary, healthy, fulfilling relationship.

Dispelling the Modern Myths About Marriage

The three most commonly held ideas about marriage today are:

1. It takes constant work to have a successful relationship.
2. Both parties in the relationship need to be committed to the success of the relationship—in other words, a good marriage is a 50/50 proposition.
3. When couples grow apart it is sufficient and legitimate cause for divorce.

Based on these three ideas, it is quite possible to find yourself feeling anxious and burdened by your relationship rather than nurtured and happy. It doesn't have to be that way. This book is based on two radical ideas that counter the current myths about marriage:

1. It only takes one person to have a healthy, happy relationship, and
2. What there is to do is a matter of fun and play, not work.

If you are willing to entertain these two possibilities, then the challenges and problems that come along—even from something as apparently fatal as growing apart—can not only be dealt with successfully but can leave you with an even stronger, closer relationship.

How This Book Came into Being

After much work and research I found and married a great guy. (This process is described in my earlier book, *How* Not *to Stay*

Single: 10 Steps to a Great Relationship, and many of the things
I learned then are included here.) Once I found Tony, I was very
intent on holding on to him. And I wasn't just interested in an
ordinary, "staying together" kind of arrangement. I wanted our
relationship to continue to be fantastic, romantic, and passionate. But my track record in relationships didn't give me much
confidence I could pull it off, so I set out on a mission to discover
the secrets of successful relationships.

I started by talking to couples who not only had been together
for a long time but were still happily married. When I asked
them their secrets, many of them gave me the same answer:
"Don't go to bed angry at each other." Although I considered
this great advice, it simply was not sufficient. I knew more went
into the making of a fulfilling relationship than this one rule. I
decided to dig deeper.

Rather than just interviewing happily married couples, I
began to observe them. I also formulated questions that brought
out more information. My marriage is a testament to how well
this process worked and how valuable it has been. Tony and
I have been married for fifteen years, and each year is more
incredible than the last. We have been through the tests of losing
our parents, infertility, adopting two children, terrific financial
gain, and later financial trouble. Through all of this, we've gotten closer and continued to have fun, exciting, and passionate
lives.

I have learned that when I slack off and don't do the things I
know I should do to keep our marriage great, it soon becomes
boring and lifeless. Fortunately, I now know exactly what to do
to get it back into shape. And with this book, you, too, will
understand how to apply the same knowledge in your own relationship. It will show you what to do in response to those problems that seem to "pop up out of nowhere." It will teach you to

identify the red flags so that you can keep many problems from developing. You will have the skills and tools to steer the relationship through storms and doldrums rather than riding them out or losing the relationship completely.

Don't Get Real, Get Radical

For more than ten years I have been giving seminars for singles called "How *Not* to Stay Single." The seminars have been very successful, and many participants have found mates. Some of them have come back to me with the question: "Now that I've found someone, what do I do with him/her?" In response, I developed a five-week course for couples called "The Art and Science of Extraordinary Relationships." I've been giving this course for seven years. This book is based on my own experience as well as the hundreds of couples I have worked with over the years. And like my course, it is built around the two radical ideas of play and responsibility.

People used to get married and stay married forever. There was really no other option. Divorce was a drastic measure. A man could lose his job because of the stigma of being divorced; a woman faced poverty and scandal. So, right or wrong, good or bad, a marriage continued.

Now the pendulum has swung to the other side. We are quick to end our relationships. If you ask people today why they divorced, most will tell you either that they grew apart or that their mate was the wrong person. I believe the real culprit is neglect. The truth is that *all* relationships, even if you've found your perfect soul mate, begin to deteriorate without the care and nourishment they need to keep them healthy and alive.

Then I often hear people say, "A relationship takes a lot of *work*" or "You've got to constantly *work* on your relationship." This sounds so burdensome, so full of drudgery. In fact, "working" on your relationship is more likely to be a factor in destroying it. I'm interested in people having relationships that are fun, exciting, challenging, passionate, and loving. It is when these positive qualities are missing that a relationship falls apart. So, putting them back in, which is fun, is what is needed, *not work*.

I'm not saying it doesn't take time, discipline, and focus. Of course it does. But time, discipline, and focus—plus a lot of passion—are the heart of creativity and play. Instead of the struggle and effort we often associate with work, my approach calls for imagination, energy, care, and attention. Doing what it takes to have an exciting, fulfilling relationship is about designing rather than rehabilitating, playing rather than fighting, and inventing rather than compromising.

This is not some empty-headed, softhearted view of relationships. Every loving relationship will face demanding and difficult times, and will face them more than once. This is about taking on the challenge and adventure of crafting a partnership with someone, a partnership that can meet and even welcome the challenges that come along and use them to grow even closer and more loving.

And as you will see in the very first chapter, it only takes one person in a loving relationship to provide the spark and the initiative to relight the fire. So far as I know, outside of literature there are no star-crossed lovers, no couples who were meant for each other and will be effortlessly, passionately in love until death do them part. But if you and your mate care for each other and want to be together, or even if you once cared for each other and wonder if you could again, it really only takes one of you to make it fly.

So never mind if he or she won't read this book. As *you* read it, you will discover those places where your own playfulness and spirit have lagged, where you have buried your own creativity, and settled for reminiscing about the past or fantasizing about the future instead of taking action in the present. And as you reawaken and take total responsibility for your relationship, you will notice a remarkable change in yourself, in your partner, and in your relationship.

Who Should Read This Book

After taking my couples workshop, one participant commented: "This course should be a prerequisite for getting a marriage license." This book is the answer to that need and provides the insurance that newlyweds or new couples are looking for. It is just as relevant, however, for those who want to ensure their long-term relationships will last and continue to grow and deepen.

Your relationship doesn't have to be in trouble for this book to be useful. If it is in trouble, however, this book could save it. If you are not about to get divorced but your relationship feels old and tired, this book will wake things up and make your relationship exciting and passionate again. And even if only one of you reads this book and takes it to heart, that is sufficient to make the difference.

This book is not a substitute for marriage counseling or professional therapy. It is a guide for couples who want to acquire the skills to keep their relationships in top form. If you read it and do the creative exercises at the end of each chapter, you, too, can have results in your relationship that exceed your expectations. You will have the tools to deal with whatever comes along in your relationship as well as the tools to create an extraordinary, passionate, and exciting love beyond your dreams. You, too, can have a relationship that is better than it was when you first met—not just good enough to last but profoundly nurturing and satisfying—and without having to get a new partner.

Take
Responsibility

I believe it is possible for one person to be responsible for the success of his or her relationship.

Most of the time, the word *responsibility* is used as a synonym for blame or fault. That is not what I mean. I mean responsibility as a claiming of ownership of specific matters in your life. It is a way of seeing yourself, of creating a context for your life based on choice instead of on the flow of occurrences and events you can't control.

Sidney Rittenberg is an American who was a political prisoner in China for ten years during the Cultural Revolution. While he had no control over his circumstances in prison, he nevertheless took a unique and extraordinary stand toward his predicament. He chose to live each day as if he were free, as if even within his four prison walls he could make a contribution. And he proceeded to actively live this way every day for ten years, never knowing if he would ever be released. In his memoirs he describes this period of his life as a remarkable time of education, growth, and even freedom.

Authentic responsibility exists only by choice. You never *have* to be responsible, yet the choice is always available to you. The disadvantage of assuming this kind of responsibility for your life is that you have to give up feeling victimized and blaming others. It's not easy. Even as adults, many of us would rather blame our parents and how we were raised for whatever we don't like about our lives. It often seems easier to find fault than to face things as they are and take specific actions to make them the way you would like them to be. On the plus side, if it is really true that having a great life is solely up to you, then nothing or no one outside of yourself can stop you. Of course, this is much simpler in theory than in practice.

There was a time when I was unhappy with Tony and particularly frustrated with our relationship. Tony could see I was upset and tried to find out what was wrong. I didn't want to talk, ask him anything, or take any time to be with him and work out my frustrations. I didn't want to do anything. I just wanted to be left alone. In fact, my response to Tony's probing was, "I know exactly what's wrong and I know exactly what needs to be done, but I just don't want to do it."

It is not easy to take the helm of your own existence and steer the ship. But what is the alternative? This is your life, the only one you've got. Are you going to make it worth living, or are you going to complain about all the things you think are wrong?

This Is Not a 50/50 Deal!

This prelude on responsibility is to prepare you for my premise that all it takes to assure the success of a relationship is for one member of the couple—either the man or the woman—to take on a commitment of 100 percent responsibility. Not only am I saying that the idea of marriage as a 50/50 proposition is a myth, I am also saying that it is completely ineffective and, as far as I'm concerned, the source of many divorces.

When relationships are based on the premise that "I'll do my part, if he does his," there is always a way out. Sure, if you do your "fifty" you're off the hook, and you can legitimately claim in divorce court that it was his fault, but you'll still end up single. You will "win" on the righteous scale, but you will lose your marriage.

As I quickly learned when I was a management consultant for both small and large businesses, there is too much room for things to fall between the cracks when responsibility is "shared." The result is often failure and finger-pointing. The same is true in marriage.

Do you want your marriage to work? Prove it. Be 100 percent responsible for it working. I know, "It's not fair!" You're right. It isn't fair. I also wish it weren't true, but I would not be completely honest if I told you what everyone else is telling you. Fifty-fifty doesn't work, and taking that path is the surefire way to divorce court.

While it is hypothetically possible for a marriage to flourish when one person is 100 percent responsible and the other 0 percent, I believe it is equivalent to experiencing freedom in a Chinese prison—possible, but pretty tough.

The ideal is for both partners to take on 100 percent responsibility, but that isn't essential. Anything in between works, as long as at least one member of the couple is holding on to 100 percent. Remember, I'm not saying it must add up to 100 percent. This is not a mathematics exercise. In fact, it can't even be 70/80. The only thing that will guarantee the relationship functioning at its maximum potential is when one partner goes the whole way—not 99.9 but the full 100 percent.

It Takes More Than Just Saying It

One of the problems with the 100 percent standard is that even when someone is willing to be fully responsible, they may not have the capability. For instance, you don't give a two-year-old the responsibility of taking care of her three-month-old sister. The two-year-old may be quick to volunteer, but obviously, she is not yet prepared for the task.

The purpose of this book is to give you the tools and skills you need to take on this extraordinary pledge. If you read and put into practice all the assignments, you will have the necessary credentials. All that will be left is to take the absolute position or stand that *you* are the one who is 100 percent responsible for your marriage.

If you choose to take this stand, you will never find yourself alone asking, "What happened? What went wrong?" Nor will you ever be the victim. If something isn't working in your marriage, you will know where to point your finger—straight at yourself.

This is not a foreign concept in our lives. As a parent, even before the baby is born, you know you are and will always be totally responsible for this precious and fragile being. It is also common to know that you are totally responsible for your business or job, the care of your parents, or the upkeep of your home. You even know you are responsible for cleaning up after your dog.

"But," you argue, "these are areas of my life that affect me personally. Everyone knows that in relationships it takes 'two to tango.'" Which only brings us back to the "it's not fair" argument. It isn't fair. It is also not a matter of negotiation. This is *not* "I'll be 100 percent responsible if you will be, too." I'm sorry; it won't fly. We're looking for total accountability.

At the beginning of the chapter, I hope I made it clear that responsibility is a choice. You can't *make* someone else responsible. You can give them responsibility, but it becomes real only when they're willing to take it on. Those of us who are parents know this well. You can't cram responsibility down your children's throats and expect them to all of a sudden take it on and keep their rooms clean without you ever having to ask again. In the same way, you can't *make* your spouse be responsible either.

It Is a Matter of Integrity

Only when *you* are freely and happily willing to take on and be the "one" responsible for your relationship can you truly make a commitment to your spouse and your marriage.

In this age of rampant divorce, commitments have apparently become cheap and meaningless. This is not something we as a culture are proud of. There is so much resistance among single men to commitment, it has given rise to a new area of study in relationships called "commitment phobia." Working with single people, it is apparent to me that one cause of this phenomena is that men don't want to give their word when they know there is better than a 50 percent chance that someday they will break it. Their "phobia" might more accurately be seen as a fear of failing, or violating their personal integrity.

Wedding vows usually conclude with the words *till death do us part,* yet few marriages last long enough to come to that end. Instead, the last words are "See you in court." I think we need to bring more reality and authenticity to the vows we take. They should be changed to reflect the truth. They could say, "I promise to stay with you until we 'grow apart,' or unless you gain weight." Or "I will stay with you unless you become an alcoholic or you cheat on me." Or how about "I will love you forever unless you harm me or my children or you do anything else I find reprehensible and unforgivable." Not very romantic vows, nor would they sound suitable at an expensive and formal church service, but they would be more honest.

Eliminate the Alternatives

I suggest an alternative—one I believe to be much more powerful and empowering. This is not an idea, however, for the faint of heart.

First of all, consider "commitment" to be an action that eliminates the "way out" or the back door. In other words, take away the "if it doesn't work out, we can always get divorced." I am saying this is what true commitment is: the elimination of *all* alternatives, even the emergency exits.

But now we're back to square one, face-to-face with the possibility of being trapped in a relationship that is unhealthy, unhappy, or even abusive—or any of the other reasons divorce was ever invented.

The solution is to take the vow one step beyond "I will stay with you no matter what," and commit to the quality of life you want by vowing something like: "I promise to have our relationship be loving, powerful, passionate, and nurturing *no matter what.*" Or even further, include, "I promise you will *want* to stay with me and I will *want* to stay with you."

As I said, this is not for the weak or insecure. But if you want to have a guaranteed, lasting, legendary relationship, first close the door and then obligate yourself with these vows. The bottom line is: "Since I can't get out of this relationship, I need to make it work."

I am not saying divorce doesn't have its place or that it should be abolished. What I am saying is that by eliminating it as an option, you will be forced to find or create the tools you need to survive and flourish as a couple.

Two of the role-model couples I interviewed for this book answered the question "What are your secrets for a successful marriage?" with "Never mention the word *divorce*." Both couples agreed fighting and disagreements may be inevitable, but they never use or threaten with the word *divorce*. As one of the women put it, "Murder, maybe—divorce, *never*."

Those of you who are divorced may be defensive at this point. "Well, what should I have done, stayed with a woman who was an alcoholic and beat our children?" Of course not. You know if you really did the right thing by getting a divorce. I have no reason not to believe you nor do I have any argument with your choice. And I'm not saying anything that happened was your fault. I am saying there is something different available in your present relationship if you are willing to take on total responsibility.

Commitment Is the Source of Inspiration

"Okay, so how do I do this?" you ask. That is what this book is about—having your relationship succeed under any and all circumstances!

But the second part of the answer, though less concrete, is more important. If you have made a "no matter what" promise in your marriage, and you have taken on a 100 percent commitment to that promise, you *will* find the way. If all of my advice doesn't work, you will get help from someone else, read more books, take courses, ask your spouse's mother what worked for her. In other words, you will do whatever it takes.

Until one is committed
there is hesitancy, the chance to draw back,
always ineffectiveness.
Concerning all acts of initiative (and creation),
there is one elementary truth,
the ignorance of which kills countless ideas
and splendid plans:
that the moment one definitely commits oneself,
then providence moves too.
All sorts of things occur to help one that would never
     otherwise have occurred.
A whole stream of events issues from the decision,
raising in one's favor all manner
of unforeseen incidents and meetings
and material assistance, which one could not have
     dreamt
would have come their way.

I have learned a deep respect
for one of Goethe's couplets:

"Whatever you can do, or dream you can, begin it.
Boldness has genius, power and magic in it."
                                        —Rudolf Steiner

Most of the important accomplishments in life begin before
everything is in place to guarantee their success, whether it is
having children or declaring an intention to be the first nation to
reach the moon. We throw our commitment out ahead of ourselves, and then go to work on the "how to." When we run out of
ready ideas or solutions to problems, it just means we will have
to invent them.

Even with this attitude, failure is still a possibility. But the probability of divorce when you don't give 100 percent is 55 to 60 percent. Surely, taking on total responsibility is going to put a major dent in this statistic.

No Matter What

At the last session of my couples course, I ask each participant to tell me what it would take for them to leave the relationship. I am now asking the same of you. More specifically, "fast forward" your marriage to a hypothetical time of divorce, and explain what would have caused the breakup.

I am looking for very precise answers to this question. I am not looking for examples of things you could never put up within a relationship.

Personally, I could never stay married to a bigot, or a murderer, or a drug addict, or someone who beat me. And Tony would never engage in any of these behaviors, but there are behaviors or attitudes he could develop that would definitely push me away and perhaps even destroy the love I feel for him. I can see this as something that potentially could happen, because it already does in small and temporary increments. For example, I think the possibility exists of him ceasing communication, becoming totally obsessed with his business, or ignoring me and withholding his attention and affection. And if it continued on a long-term or permanent basis, I would want out of the marriage.

So, I ask everyone in the class, as I am now asking you, what could you imagine your partner doing that would warrant you leaving. Now tell your partner what it is.

Not surprisingly, everyone knows exactly what to say. Sheila said she would leave Richard if he started to drink again, continued drinking, and stopped attending AA meetings. Stephen said he would leave Carol if she cheated on him. Barbara said she would leave if Tim was physically abusive to her or their children. Don said he wouldn't be able to stand it if Judith stopped wanting to make love.

Once couples know what it is—and now that you and your spouse know as well—*you* make the promise that your spouse will not do the thing you said you'd leave them for.

My promise is Tony will not withdraw and he will always be willing to communicate. Sheila promises Richard will remain sober and attend meetings. Stephen promises Carol will not have an affair. Barbara promises Tim will never be abusive. And Don promises Judith will always genuinely desire to make love to him.

But What If . . . ?

How can you make a promise for another's actions? Let me answer with another question: How could Sidney Rittenberg promise to live as a free man in prison? Or how could President John Kennedy promise our nation would be first in the race to the moon?

When you are willing to be responsible, you find the way. For myself, I have found that the way I am with Tony has the effect of either inviting his communication or shutting him off. And I always have to remember two very important things: (1) we're on the same side—he *likes* to communicate just as much as I do, and (2) when I attack and blame him, it usually produces a negative result (surprise, surprise).

Certainly you can't control the thinking and behavior of another person, and manipulation breeds disrespect, which will sabotage a relationship in other ways. But you always have a choice of either giving power to or taking power away from your spouse and your relationship. The more often you choose to empower, the stronger and more secure your relationship will be.

It takes courage to be responsible for your life—to give up blaming your parents, society, the institution of marriage, and of course, your spouse. Either way, you get to live with the fruits of your labors. If you choose to be responsible, you can have a marriage that is not only fulfilling beyond belief, but nurturing to yourself and your immediate family and an inspiration and blueprint for others. What you have to give up is nothing compared to what you receive in return—waking up each day to a life of bliss.

Exercises in Creating What You Want

A. What are the underlying or undeclared vows in your marriage? For example, "I'll stay unless you are unfaithful [hit me, bore me, gain too much weight, lose your hair, etc.]."

B. Are you willing to be 100 percent responsible for your marriage? What does this mean to you? Who would you have to stop blaming or holding responsible for the problems in your relationship?

C. What about your spouse would cause you to leave?

D. What vows or promises are you now willing to make?

Stop Focusing
on What's Wrong and
Start Getting
What You Want

Most loving relationships begin with two people in wild appreciation and adoration of each other. But over time many deteriorate to the point where the couple can only speak about their marriage in terms of what doesn't work.

I've asked couples to describe what their relationships were like when they first got together. Instead of telling me how in love they were, they tell me all the things that were wrong: we were very young; we thought we had to be married to live together; we didn't really know each other; all our friends were getting married, so we did, too. But I don't buy this. I don't believe that these people were so stupid as to marry someone they didn't love. These weren't shotgun weddings. These people got married because they were in love—maybe immature, but still in love.

The first step to the rebirth of a relationship is to remember who and what you fell in love with.

A few years ago, Bob and Sharon, a couple who complained that their relationship was not only not working but was dead, came to my seminar. They weren't ready to leave each other, they said, nor were they having affairs. There just wasn't any life left in their eighteen-year marriage. I asked them to tell me what was great, what was the best thing about their relationship. "We don't bother each other. We let the other do whatever he or she wants," they said. Their mutually shared focus on staying out of each other's way was the *best thing* they had to say about their marriage!

I made them dig deeper to tell me what it was like when they were first together. After a few moments of hesitation and struggle they began to remember how much fun they used to have. Sharon told me about Bob's playfulness and several of his practical jokes. Bob recalled what a buddy she was; she was a great sport and was up for anything. Soon they began to get back in touch with the qualities that had attracted them to each other in the first place. By the end of the seminar both of them had rediscovered wonderfully stimulating and lovable aspects of the other. So much so that Bob was bragging about how much fun she was and you could see the passion had returned to their marriage.

The Order of Things to Come

There is a natural progression or, more accurately, regression in any relationship. You fall in love with someone and everything about them is wonderful, miraculous, enchanting. You love the way he is with his family, the way he listens to you. The way she tilts her head is so graceful, and you love her mischievousness. You are endlessly fascinated and enthralled with every movement, every touch. And you express the thrill of it all. You tell your new love how sensitive and special he is. You tell your parents and your friends that she is the most warm and giving woman you've ever met.

You know how nauseatingly people go on and on when they're first in love? Family and friends put up with it because they know it will pass. And sure enough it does. And then something happens, or an imperfection peeks through. She's always late, or he watches too much television. In a way, even this stage feels good at first—as if having a problem to work out is a signal that this is a relationship to take seriously. When your friends ask you how things are going you can say, "Great, but we have a few issues we need to work on."

Everything is as it should be, except for this "one thing." This is where we decide that what it's going to take to make everything perfect again is work. This is also where appreciation begins to take a backseat to our efforts to make everything fit our ideas of how we think it should be. And more often than not, this is the beginning of the end of a great relationship.

You don't have to do anything about the good things because "if it ain't broke, don't fix it," right? So you devote lots of attention to this problem-thing. You discuss it with each other, you read books about it, and you seek advice from friends. Meanwhile, less and less of your attention goes to those great qualities you fell head-over-heels in love with, the reasons you got married in the first place. There seems to be an unspoken agreement that you don't need to pay attention to "how generous she is" or "how sensitive he is." Those qualities are fine; they don't need any correction or improvement.

Eventually, we are only paying attention to the problems. And since problems get the focus, problems are all we see and experience. The nonproblematic things we used to dote on, the things that enamored us, fade far into the background from lack of attention.

This is how we take a fulfilling, nurturing, exciting relationship and kill it. Almost everyone does it, too. Proof of point: How many lively and passionate longtime relationships do *you* know of?

Use It or Lose It

What is not appreciated does not last. We all know the story about the attractive woman who gets married and then lets her looks go. The usual line of gossip is that she only took care of herself to get married. I find this isn't usually the case.

The good-looking woman who keeps herself fit and well groomed discovers early in her relationship that her boyfriend or fiancé likes this about her. He compliments her looks, her new hairstyle, or how great that dress looks on her. She blossoms from his attention. His expressions of admiration make her feel attractive and loved and she makes sure she continues to look great because he notices.

After a period of time, however, probably well after the wedding, he starts taking her beauty for granted and stops paying attention to how she looks. He is happy to see her at the end of the day but rarely compliments her on her appearance. One day she comes home with a new hair color, and he doesn't even comment. Soon after, she begins to think it's no big deal if she wears the sweat suit she's been wearing all day, or if she doesn't wash her hair as often. He doesn't notice anyway. Next, she starts skipping her workout—also no big deal.

She doesn't put much effort into how she looks anymore because it doesn't seem to matter. And because her attractiveness is no longer acknowledged, there is no longer any of the original pleasure or reward for her.

Nothing is mentioned about her appearance again until the day he notices the emergence of some new growth in her hips. *Then* he speaks up, telling her "she's got some new fenders on her chassis." So now, because once upon a time he expressed his admiration for her looks in glowing compliments and attentive remarks, but has said nothing for a long time, and has just criticized her with a wisecrack, there is a "problem." *He* has lost the beauty he cherished, and *she* has lost her appreciative and sensitive man (not to mention slim hips).

It is a red flag signaling trouble when something that was once wonderful in a relationship begins to disappear. This is a wake-up call that you have been taking your spouse for granted. Immediate attention is required.

Sometime back I appeared on a morning talk show in Houston while on tour promoting my last book. After the show, the producer came up to introduce himself and thank me. This man was one of the most sexy, magnificent-looking men I had ever laid eyes on. So, when he asked if he could attend the seminar I had scheduled for that night, I said yes, of course. (Are you kidding!) As it turned out, he later left a message saying that he wouldn't be able to make the seminar, but he would like to meet me afterward and take me to dinner.

When I got home the next day my husband, Tony, asked me about the trip, and I told him I went to dinner with the TV producer and almost got in trouble.

"And how did the show go?" Tony asked, to which I replied, "Tony! Wrong question! I just told you I had dinner with a man and almost got in trouble."

I travel alone all over the world. I work with and see lots of men. Almost never do they come on to me. It's not that I'm unattractive. It's just that I don't put out the vibes that invite advances. I did, however, in Houston.

Tony finally got the point. And so did I. I was looking around because he had not gotten his job done, the job of paying me the kind of attention that makes me feel attractive and desirable. I needed to feel I was attractive and sexy, and Tony was the one I really wanted to make me feel that way. Furthermore, if Tony forgot to do his job, then it was up to me to ask him directly to do it—not try to remind him by flirting, or worse.

This is a good example of the kind of "problem" we could have worked on. Instead, we saw that we simply had been neglecting our expressions of affection and appreciation for each other. Restoring those qualities to our relationship was not something either of us considered work; it was quick, easy, and fun.

If It Ain't Broke . . . Love It!

If it helped to focus on what doesn't work in a relationship, I would support it as a method for dealing with the issues that inevitably arise in relationships. But it simply doesn't work! It doesn't solve problems or make things better.

I know couples who have been together forty years, and the same complaints between them are still rampant—he's always late and doesn't communicate, and she still spends too much money. Years of critical attention and focus haven't changed the problems at all, except perhaps to have made them bigger. Problems have become the core of these relationships and any delight with one another has long since wasted away.

Patterns or habits of taking each other for granted can set in early in a relationship. Tony and I had been together about a year when he came home from work one evening, kissed me, and sat down with the newspaper. I sat next to him and watched him read. After a few minutes, I took the paper and put it aside. Then I took his hand and walked him out the front door.

"We are going to do this again," I said. "I refuse to spend evening after evening *watching* you read the paper. You happen to be very lucky to live with me, and if you don't treat this relationship as special and express how fortunate you are, you don't get to keep it. Now, walk in again and show me that you're thrilled to see me, that you feel lucky to be with me. And show me all of this without looking as if I'm an obstacle on your way to the newspaper."

Tony told me that he realized what had happened in his first marriage from this interaction. To the observer, Tony had been the nice guy in the marriage, his wife was the shrew, and he was smart to leave her. But he had taken the marriage for granted and had neglected it in the same way he was in danger of doing with our relationship.

The Blue Plate Special

Walk into a small-town cafe or roadside diner, and you're likely to see the daily Blue Plate Special printed on a chalkboard above the cash register. For one low price you get a main course— let's say corned beef and cabbage with maybe side dishes of green beans and mashed potatoes—coffee or tea, and probably pudding or, if it's a really great place, homemade pie for dessert.

Always, under the description of that day's special, are the words *No Substitutions!* If you order the Blue Plate Special, you agree to take the whole meal as described. You cannot substitute corn for the green beans, rice for the potatoes, cake for the pudding. I know you think the waiter or waitress should make an exception for you, but the good ones don't. You either take the Blue Plate Special the way it comes on the menu, or you order something else.

Every relationship is like a Blue Plate Special. When we fall in love, we go for the succulent corned beef and we think, this is great. Corned beef is just what I want. And when we see a flaw or imperfection, then we say, if only I could do something to change these green beans everything would be perfect. I just don't like green beans. So we set out to cajole, plead, bribe— anything to get rid of the green beans.

The pitfall is that we spend so much time trying to change what can't be changed that we never get around to enjoying the main course. Instead of taking the green beans and leaving them on the plate while we enjoy the luscious corned beef, we keep trying to change the Blue Plate Special to match our taste. We allow a great main course to grow cold and inedible while we whine like children about the vegetables we don't like.

Instead of enjoying intimacy and closeness with our spouses, we squander precious time and energy trying to get her to be more organized or him to be neater. Instead of deciding we can live with habitual lateness and delighting in a partner who adores us, we nag our way into divorce court. As far as I can tell, just as there are no substitutions on the Blue Plate Special, there are no flawless partners. You don't get to change what you don't like on the Blue Plate Special, and you don't get to change what you don't like in your partner.

I consider this one of the greatest sins in relationships. We so quickly take our partner's wonderful qualities for granted and then let those qualities deteriorate and go to waste by not appreciating them. Meanwhile we spend countless hours, years, decades trying to change their modest imperfections, when what we should have been doing all along is admiring and basking in the glories of this magnificent person.

Spread the Good News

The bad news is that almost all of us do this. The good news is it is easy to correct. Whatever gets our focus, gets our energy and power. If you focus on flaws, mistakes, and imperfections, then those weaknesses grow. On the other hand, if you focus on strengths and talents, then those qualities grow. I learned this principle when I first began training others to do what I had been doing successfully for some time, conducting time management seminars for corporations.

My first group of trainees had to stand in front of the group for twenty minutes at a time and practice leading a seminar while I observed and scribbled very astute and detailed notes, which of course consisted of all their mistakes. Afterward I let them know what I had found wrong with their work so they could improve: you didn't speak loudly enough; you didn't make the point clearly; you never answered Arnie's question.

After a few hours of work, however, instead of improving, my trainees could barely utter two sentences in front of the group. I was sure I had an inept bunch, but I asked a more experienced trainer to sit in on my session just to verify that I had a slow group. He identified the problem right away. And it wasn't my trainees. He explained that because I was only pointing out flaws and mistakes, their inadequacies were getting more pronounced. "Everyone has weak points that need improvement," he said, "that's a given. However, if you work only on their imperfections, they're not going to improve."

He encouraged me to use my perceptive and critical skills to bring about the opposite outcome. "Work on their strengths, and they will blossom," he said. "They'll never be perfect, but if you nurture their strong points, they will grow stronger. *Eventually, their strengths will overshadow their weaknesses.*"

In my next session, I made sure to tell the trainees the things they did right: it was great the way you got Joe's attention; you knew the material well; your joke really broke the ice. The difference was remarkable—big improvements showed up right away. Once they achieved some confidence and trusted that I was on their side and wanted them to succeed, they readily began to fix the aspects of their work that needed correction. They were able to incorporate my suggestions for changes and, instead of shutting down, started to improve and succeed.

The same is true with couples who have taken my course. When I ask them to describe what they fell in love with, they begin to open up, often after a long time of being shut down. Each person gets to listen to their spouse say things that have long gone unsaid and unremembered: "This was the best-looking man I had ever seen." "I knew she would always be honest, she oozed integrity." "No one has ever made me laugh the way he did." "Her sense of adventure grabbed me—I knew life would never be boring."

As each spouse opens up and drinks in the love and attraction, the couple become more beautiful and full of fun and passion right before our eyes. "Oldy weds" who had actually forgotten these feelings ever existed rediscover them. When they express them to each other as they did when they first fell in love, they become alive and vibrant again.

I don't mean to say that problems don't exist and don't need some attention. We will handle those "how-tos" in later chapters. But like the example of my seminar leader trainees, when you have a solid foundation of expressed love, adoration, devotion, and appreciation, problem solving and correction come much more naturally and easily. Use your attention to empower what is working, what is wonderful about your partner.

Exercises in Creating What You Want

If your partner is resistant or uninterested, do not shy away
from doing these exercises yourself. They are so validating and
empowering, your partner will eventually want to participate.

Write down your responses to the following questions and
then read them to your partner. Be totally positive. No back-
handed compliments. This means censor the "buts." No "He always used to talk about his day with me, *but* stopped when . . . !"
Delete the "but" and everything that might come after it.

   A. Describe what it was about your spouse that made
       you fall in love. What were the qualities, mannerisms,
       values that attracted you?

   B. How were you two together? What did you do? Why
       was it fun? What made being together special? Excit-
       ing? Passionate? What did you talk about? What did
       you feel like when you were together?

   C. When did you know you were in love? Describe the
       situation. When was it? What happened?

Stop the Sabotage

Why is it that some people do not get married because they fear it will ruin their relationship? What is it about "marriage" that causes this fear? More to the point, why is it often true that a good relationship *does* begin to die at the altar?

As far as I can see, there is nothing in most marriage vows that dictates a changed behavior or forces you to do things you don't want to do. Yet something happens, something changes as soon as the rings go on the fingers—and it is often not desirable.

I am speaking of the changes we blame on marriage itself— husband always takes out the garbage, wife is the cook and goes to PTA meetings, husband earns more than wife, husband no longer goes out with the guys, married couples give up their opposite-sex friendships, married couples have to spend weekends and holidays together. In other words, getting married means you settle down, get old, boring, stuffy, and, in general, stop having fun.

I remember telling my father that Tony and I were going trekking in Peru on our honeymoon. I have always been an avid adventure traveler and this seemed like a natural and exciting trip to take together. My father's response was, "But I thought you were getting married," as if getting married meant I would no longer travel as I used to.

The changes we make after marriage are often not thoughtful decisions but, more likely, unconscious ones, and the resulting unwanted and destructive behavior seems out of our control. We find ourselves saying or doing things totally out of character. For instance, often I notice my mother's words coming out of my mouth and then, shocked, I look down at myself as though I've been possessed. It's as if "Marriage made me do it."

Where Did That Come From?

Marriage can be heaven; it can also be hell. Most marriages fall somewhere in the middle with love, support, and generosity mixed in with the occasional criticism, resentment, and nagging. But "marriage" doesn't determine this, you do!

From the time you were a small child, you've been collecting tidbits of information on male/female relationships from two primary sources: fantasy and reality. What you haven't been doing is screening this information very carefully, so your conclusions are bound to get you into trouble.

On the fantasy side, we are all prone to the "happily ever after" end of most fairy tales, novels, and movies. But most of the fairy tales, novels, and movies from which we select our information are the ones that *end* with the marriage. It's no wonder that many newlywed couples look at each other the day after the honeymoon and think, "Now what?" It is not uncommon for depression to set in after the glow of the wedding wears off and the couples are left feeling as if something wonderful is over rather than something wonderful has just begun.

On the reality side, things are often not much better. All your life, you have observed your family, relatives, and neighbors and unwittingly used them as role models. Because most of them weren't exactly doing a terrific job relating, you have collected a number of bad attitudes.

If you were exposed to an abusive relationship or one in which negative qualities were the norm, you probably developed a bad attitude toward the whole institution. But you didn't have to grow up on the set of *Who's Afraid of Virginia Woolf?* to end up with negative attitudes about relationships. Even in a happy home, there is ample opportunity for a child to learn about the darker side of male/female unions.

Most likely your parents had a fight or two in front of you. That was all it took for you to decide relationships are full of struggles. If your mother had to account to your father for the money she spent, you might have concluded that in marriage, women answer to men, or women don't know how to handle money. And if one of your parents asked you to conceal something from the other, you got the idea that deception is normal as well.

You bring these negative attitudes, opinions, and fears with you to your marriage, and they play a large part in determining what your marriage will be like. There is the "men are babies" mantra you learned from your Aunt Viola. Or your dad's macho adage, "Real men don't even know where the kitchen is." You might have come up with one of your own: "Marriage is a 50/50 proposition—you give 50 percent and they take the other 50."

Who Cooks?

My friends Sarah and Tom got married after living together for four years. Five months after the wedding, Sarah called to tell me she was ready to quit. She hated being married, she said; it had ruined the wonderful relationship she had with Tom.

I asked her what the problem was. She said Tom had the nerve to come home the night before and ask, "Where's dinner?" Sarah lost her temper, telling Tom she was not his slave, and she'd like to know when was the last time *he* thought of cooking dinner.

She was really shocked at him, because during all their years of living together, they would both come home from work and talk about what to do for dinner. Sometimes she cooked, sometimes he did, sometimes they went out. "Now, just because we're married," she said, "I'm supposed to have dinner on the table every night like a good little wife?"

I delved further to find out what had been happening since the wedding. Had she been doing a lot more of the cooking? "Well, yes," she said. "I got into the whole scene. I wanted to try all the wonderful kitchen presents we got. And I really got into the wife thing, preparing gourmet romantic dinners." She, in fact, had cooked almost every night without any discussion with Tom about it. And she had enjoyed it.

"First," I said, "let's lay off Tom. If someone had cooked for me every night for five months, I would expect dinner to be there, too. The real focus belongs on you. How come, after four years together, you suddenly started cooking every night?"

That's when Sarah realized she had an unconscious belief: The wife does the cooking. It wasn't written into the marriage contract. Tom hadn't demanded it of her (although he sure got used to it real quick). Sarah had brought her belief into the marriage, and because it was unconscious, it was never discussed. Who would do the cooking or what to do about dinner was never negotiated because her unconscious edict was: The wife is the cook. When Sarah got tired of living out her own belief and felt its constraints, she rebelled against Tom instead of the self-inflicted regulation.

Who Spends the Money?

A personal experience of how unconscious beliefs influenced my own relationship occurred soon after Tony and I were married. I had been on my own, self-sufficient and financially independent for years before meeting Tony. But as soon as Tony and I married and combined our money, I began checking with him before making purchases for anything other than everyday items such as groceries. Whenever I wanted a new outfit or something new for our condo, I'd tell him about it and ask if it was okay to spend the money.

Tony is very generous and always said yes. The first time he said no was one time when he didn't think I needed another pair of boots. I hit the ceiling! "What do you mean?" I said. "Who are you to tell me whether or not I can spend money? This is my money, too! I don't have to ask *you* every time I spend a penny!"

Tony just stood there looking at me calmly and said, "Then why did you?"

It didn't take long for me to catch on. I realized I had cast Tony and myself in roles my mother and father had played in their marriage. Tony had never told me I had to ask him before making a purchase. It was my idea to be accountable to him because that was how my mother behaved with my father.

This was a requirement that I had unwittingly brought into the marriage, assuming it was what married women do. As soon as it came to the surface, I realized how unnatural it was for Tony and me to behave this way. I never asked permission to spend money again. More to the point, by discovering and then letting go of our unconscious beliefs and regulations, Tony and I have designed our own way of dealing with money, rather than being hostage to a system created by our parents. (More about dealing with money in a later chapter.)

Many of the bad attitudes you formed about marriage came from observing the sadness and frustrations of your parents. Even if your parents had a wonderful and inspiring relationship, it may not be useful as a role model for marriage today. That was then and this is now. But you soaked it up. And not just how they were in their marriage, but also every cultural, generational, and personal point of view they held about men and women. And when you grew up and noticed that the world had changed, did you go back and revise these views? No, you didn't even question whether they still applied. You just plopped them down in the middle of your relationship, then wondered why it looked the way it did.

Later, your own relationships became the source of negative attitudes. Whenever you experienced frustration, anger, jealousy, or loss, you racked up dozens of new negative conclusions. If you went through a divorce, you added even more to your already extensive collection of pessimistic beliefs. And along with that lingering sense of disillusionment and failure came decisions like, "I need to take care of me first," or "I'm not going to be taken advantage of again."

Expose Your Attitudes

You, however, don't live in the restricted world of your parents and grandparents. You don't even live in the world of your last relationship or marriage. You have choices and options. But to the extent that your hidden, unquestioned attitudes are dictating your behavior, they are limiting the choices you can make. If your behavior is controlled by the negative attitudes and decisions you've made in the past, *you are reacting instead of making your own choices.* To make choices, you have to release the hold these attitudes have had on you.

Exposing your negative attitudes is the first step in being able to have the kind of relationship you really want. The next step is to become aware of how these attitudes have been holding you back in your marriage. The third step is to create your own rules, beliefs, and attitudes.

The way your relationships have been turning out has been determined by you, even if that determination has been largely unconscious. Since you are the one in charge, then why not have your marriage be great, powerful, and nurturing. What this takes is to first bring the attitudes and beliefs that are presently running the show to the surface, and then sort out the ones you want to keep from those you wish to discard.

Not everything you learned from your past is bad. For instance, you may have a hidden belief that honesty and integrity are essential to a good marriage. When you bring this to the surface, you also realize that this is a belief you want to maintain as part of your relationship makeup, so you keep it.

Once this sorting out process is complete, look for other ingredients to add to your principles for a great partnership. For example, perhaps you want to add the following:

- Being married allows me greater freedom to be myself.
- Marriage provides a foundation of love that empowers all my other work.
- Being loved gives me more love to share with others.
- I can tell my spouse anything.
- Marriage gets better, more alive, more passionate with each year.

Marriage doesn't seem so limiting, restrictive, and suppressive when you start talking about it this way. The most important point here is that you are always the one designing your marriage whether you like it or not. You can either let your unconscious attitudes and beliefs be in charge or you can choose the ones you want. Once you realize this, the choice is obvious. The only thing required is that you stop complaining about "How marriage is" and be responsible for how you're going to make it.

Confessions of a Former Saboteur

Sometimes our unconscious attitudes and fears come in the form of "sabotage patterns"—the particular patterns and tendencies we have that damage relationships. My father used a particular Yiddish expression that I think says it all: "Everybody has a shtick."

I was shocked to discover my "shtick" one night when Tony and I were having dinner with my girlfriend Leslie only a few months after we had met.

I was proud of my new boyfriend and wanted to show him off. "Tony," I said, "tell Leslie how you got your job with the Seattle Sonics." He did, and when he finished, I filled in the parts he had left out.

A few minutes later I said, "Tony, tell Leslie that funny story you told me last night." Again he told her, and again I embellished his story with the details I thought made it more amusing and more to the point.

Before long, Leslie and I were doing all the talking. Tony was reduced to playing with objects on the table—his spoon, his water glass, his napkin, my fingers.

By the time we finished dinner I was embarrassed, angry, and upset. I thought Tony was acting like a jerk. I decided then and there that I would not continue to see him. I couldn't have a relationship with a man who acted like a child.

As we walked across the parking lot to the car, it hit me—a realization so powerful that I will never forget it. Tony had become progressively less interested in talking as the evening wore on. What I saw as childish behavior was his way of reacting to my repeated interruptions and corrections. I guess he figured it was inefficient for both of us to have to say what was on his mind.

Talk about acting like a jerk! I couldn't believe that I had suppressed him in that way. But that wasn't the end of my realization. In a flash, I saw that I had similarly suppressed every man I'd ever been with. I hadn't done it on purpose or even consciously; I had done it in such a subtle way that not only had I not seen it, no one else had seen it either. But I saw it now, and the truth was inescapable: I had sabotaged and destroyed every relationship I'd had by inhibiting and dominating the men I had gone out with.

I didn't think of it as suppression when I was doing it. I thought I was "helping them improve," or "offering useful advice." In fact, most men I dated told me I was the most perceptive woman they'd ever met. But my insights always pointed out their flaws and inadequacies. And after a steady diet of these "insights," they would inevitably lose confidence in themselves.

My explanation for this phenomenon always cast the blame on the man. "He couldn't stand up to a powerful woman," or "He couldn't handle me because I'm too smart." But in that one moment in the parking lot I saw that I had spent my life looking for a man who would not become dependent, and yet I had always found a way to bring men's weaknesses to the forefront.

For a moment I hated myself, but then the third part of the realization hit. I saw that my ability to turn men into wimps and bring out their weakness could be turned around. I could use the same power and perception to bring out the best in them. I saw that now I would finally be able to have a successful relationship.

This realization was a major turning point for me. Once I saw how I had been sabotaging my relationships, I could see how to stop doing it.

Uncover Your Shtick

Every person I have ever worked with has sabotaged his or her relationships to one degree or another. Everyone does it in their own way and often cannot see it themselves—that is, until they look for it. In every case, discovering how they did it has been the first step toward turning it around. And in the course of doing this, they discovered that they—not their mates, their circumstances, or their luck—were responsible for how their relationships turned out.

The first thing to know about your pattern of sabotage is that it is hidden. That's quite obvious, right? If you knew what you were doing to hurt your marriage, you'd stop doing it. But your method of sabotage is not just hidden, it is cleverly disguised as "what men always do," or "what keeps going wrong," or "what always happens in marriages." Or, in other words, it's not your fault.

Four Questions to Ask Yourself

1. Do I sabotage my marriage?

Do you have any sort of recurring problem, large or small, that keeps cropping up in your marriage? If you do (and I have never met anyone who doesn't), you should assume you are the one responsible for it.

You should assume this not so you can feel bad or guilty about it. It's simply that by taking the position that you are responsible, you can stop it from causing damage. This pattern or shtick may never go away completely. You just need to look for it so you can stop yourself before you create a problem, or if you have caused a problem, you can make corrections immediately. The important thing is to know what your shtick is and catch yourself before you use it.

It will always be more comfortable to describe your problem as "what keeps going wrong" or "what my wife (or husband) always does." Seeing yourself as the innocent victim is much easier than seeing yourself as the one pulling the strings. But seeing yourself as a victim is never going to make the problem go away. It may sound like bad news that you're the one causing the argument or undermining the marriage, but it's really good news. If you are the one causing the problem, you are the one who can fix it.

Accepting that you are responsible for the problems that surface in your relationship is the most difficult aspect of this process. That's because when you see what you have been doing, you feel like a jerk. It's your natural instinct to avoid being wrong at all costs, so you'll probably encounter some resistance to pointing the finger at yourself.

The moment of truth when I saw how I had destroyed relationships with men was an awful moment. Realizing that I had suppressed men did not make me feel proud of myself, but it was the key to my being able to start behaving differently in relationships.

You have two choices. You can consider yourself the victim in your marriage and continue to have the same problems you've had, or you can view your pattern as an inside job and learn how to stop repeating it.

2. Why do I sabotage relationships?

We've already seen that one reason you create problems in your marriage is because of the negative attitudes and fears you inherited from your past. Undoubtedly there are many other reasons at the root of why people undermine their marriages, but fortunately it isn't necessary for you to analyze them in order to stop doing them.

In most cases, trying to figure out "why" is just a way of avoiding coming to terms with your pattern and only leads to what is called "analysis paralysis." It wasn't necessary for me to understand all the deep, psychological reasons behind my pattern or to figure out specifically why I suppressed men, and it hasn't been necessary for any of the couples I've worked with to analyze the reasons behind their patterns.

Telling the truth about your shtick is what sets you free. Who cares why you've been screwing it up as long as you stop?

3. How do I sabotage my marriage?

This is a key question. Finding out how you do this will allow you to stop. In the next section I describe some of the most popular methods of marital sabotage, and you may recognize your own shtick among them.

If you don't find your pattern among these few examples, use them as a tool to identify your own. Look not only in your current relationship, but your past ones as well. (Our patterns tend to follow us wherever we go.)

4. How do I stop sabotaging my marriage?

Once you admit that you do it and discover how you do it, you're ready to reform. The path to rehabilitation is also described in the next section.

In the following pages, I identify five common shticks. One or more of them may apply to your situation. Each pattern is broken down into three parts: how you see it, what's really going on, and what to do about it. See if you recognize yourself in any of them.

Shtick 1

How you see it: *I feel smothered.*

Are you most attracted to your spouse when he or she seems aloof or distant? Do you lose interest when they're affectionate or act adoring? Are you easily bored? Do you get turned off when they get mushy? People with this pattern are often uncomfortable with open expressions of love and affection. They like attention and affection to be "hard to get" and difficult to come by.

What's really going on.

Contrary to what most people who have this pattern think, it has nothing to do with liking a challenge. Instead it is indicative of a case of low self-esteem—yours. As Groucho Marx once said, "I wouldn't want to belong to any club that would accept me as a member." If you have this pattern, you don't want to be in a relationship with anyone who has poor enough taste to be in love with someone like you.

But if you can't love someone who loves you, you're not going to be able to have much of a relationship.

What to do about it.

Next time your husband or wife starts being appreciative and attentive, don't run away screaming and don't pronounce him or her a bore. Instead, see if you can bring yourself to endure and learn to tolerate this experience. Give yourself a chance to see how it feels to be liked. Notice how much you want to run away, but instead of doing it, remind yourself that liking you is a sign of someone's good taste!

I once worked with a couple, Steve and Marsha, who had been married for ten years and had two children. I had never before witnessed a more verbally abusive relationship. He was not only constantly demeaning her, using the foulest language and name calling, but would often come out and flatly say he couldn't stand her and couldn't care less about her or the marriage. After witnessing a few of his outrageous and often public displays, I was amazed that Marsha was willing to stay with him for a moment longer, let alone continue on year after year. She always complained about him and was quite open about how obnoxious he was. She often threatened to leave, but she never would go through with it.

Even though I care a great deal about marriages lasting and about working with people so they find ways to resolve their problems and conflicts, I was about to strongly encourage her to get divorced. This relationship was absurd and abusive, and that is one condition I do not believe should ever be tolerated. Then I remembered that they were in my course after all, and Steve had been attending each session without fail. Although his words were awful, his presence said something about his commitment and concern.

I arranged a meeting with Steve alone. I told him I saw through his act and knew he really loved Marsha, so I couldn't understand why he treated her so abominably. He broke down in tears and confessed he acted that way because he was terrified she would leave him otherwise. It was his experience that whenever he showed his real love for her, she lost interest—so much so that one time she admitted to having an affair.

He was in a double bind. He had to treat the woman he was crazy about like dirt, because if he expressed his true feelings she would lose interest and leave.

Marsha had the "I don't want to be smothered" pattern. This is an example of how unhealthy a marriage can become when this pattern is taken to its extreme. In this case, more than my course was needed, so I referred the couple to therapy. They are now doing fabulously.

It's also interesting to note how most of us would have thought that Steve was the problem. It appeared as if Marsha was the victim, right? Steve's behavior was horribly inappropriate, but the key to unlocking their struggle was when Marsha discovered it was her shtick that was the source of Steve's actions.

Shtick 2

How you see it: *I give more than I get.*

Are you always the one who "gives" in your marriage? Do you feel as if you are always there with patience, understanding, and kindness when it's needed, but you never get this treatment in return?

What's really going on.

Doormats say "Welcome" on them, and every martyr has to have a persecutor. If this is your pattern, you are not happy unless you're treated less well than you treat others, so you manipulate others into doing just that.

To keep your partner from being as good as you are, you ask him to do things for you when you know he has no time. Or you ask in such an accusatory way that he has to say no. When he does try to do things for you, you don't react graciously, you complain that whatever he did wasn't done right.

True giving is free and is done for the giver's pleasure. If you're keeping score, you're not giving.

What to do about it.

It's important for you to keep a close watch on your actions in order to resist your tendency to "give" as a means of manipulating. When you do give, don't keep score. Stop looking at what he or she is doing or not doing for you. When someone *does* something nice, even something small, be appreciative.

Shtick 3

How you see it: *My spouse says we have a problem, and I don't see it.*

Are you always surprised when your spouse is unhappy? When a problem is brought up you may say, "Oh, honey, that's really nothing. I'm sure it will blow over. Don't worry so much." After all, you're sure that *you* would never do anything that annoys—*you* never nag or expect too much. And you're always careful to avoid conflict.

What's really going on.

People with this pattern have their heads buried in the sand. Barry was the classic ostrich. His first wife left him suddenly. For him, her departure "came out of the blue." He speculated that she left him because she was going through a midlife crisis. But his new wife was beginning to sound the same. He was even surprised that she thought they needed to take my course.

What he realized in my seminar was that by avoiding conflict, he had not addressed any of the problems that existed in the relationship. He thought if he ignored them they would go away, but of course they didn't.

With his unwillingness to communicate about anything uncomfortable, there wasn't much to talk about. So much was avoided there was nothing left to share. His "don't rock the boat" attitude made his relationships boring and mundane.

What to do about it.

Start noticing when you want to ignore the issues that arise in your marriage. Stop letting them go by. When your discomfort threatens to keep you from communicating, remind yourself what refusing to confront issues will cost you. When your spouse says there is a problem, take it seriously. Stop whatever you are doing and give the matter your immediate attention. Your efforts to trivialize it will only make matters worse.

Shtick 4

How you see it: *Your husband or wife is threatened by your power.*

Does your spouse think your opinions are better than his or her own? Do you feel your strength is overpowering? Are you supportive? Always offering helpful advice? Do you tend to become an "adviser" to your spouse to the point he or she can't do anything without your input?

What's really going on.

This, as you may recall, is my pattern. I tried to "help" men by pointing out how they could improve and by constantly correcting them. If you have this pattern, you probably consider yourself to be very perceptive. You think you are using your insight to help in your marriage, but what you're actually doing is constantly finding and pointing out your spouse's faults. The message your spouse is getting from you, however subtle, is that he (or she) is not okay.

Your husband probably did fine without you. However, once you became a devoted couple he became dependent. He stopped making decisions, because he knows you'll only reverse them. He may have become addicted to your advice. And as he has lost self-confidence, he has become less and less attractive to you.

What to do about it.

Start using your intelligence and perceptiveness to build your spouse or wife up instead of dragging him or her down. For example, if she asks you "What do you think?" instead of giving your usually brilliant answer, ask her what she thinks. Then when she tells you, just shut up and listen. At first, you may have trouble trusting her ideas and responses, because you are so used to your way being the best way. Don't be surprised, though, if the solutions she comes up with are better than yours. Learn to trust her decisions—after all, it was her competence and self-assurance that attracted you in the first place.

Shtick 5

How you see it: *You have become a wimp in the marriage.*

Does all the ease and confidence you feel in your professional life fly out the window the minute you are around your spouse? Do you avoid saying what is on your mind because you are worried you'll look pushy? Do you feel needy and clingy? Do you become intensely focused on the relationship? Do you feel insecure every time you are apart?

What's really going on.

You are dependent on your partner for your identity. You're "nobody till somebody loves you." You can probably point to a long list of accomplishments and professional successes to prove how independent you are, but underneath you feel you need your spouse's approval just to feel all right.

If you're like most people who have this pattern, you seem anything but dependent. In fact, it is your fear of dependency that motivates you to put so much energy into your career. Your achievements are a way of compensating for the desperation you feel about your relationship.

What to do about it.

You're so used to covering up your feelings of desperation about needing someone that just admitting you are this way is a great step forward. Next time you notice the desperate or "clingy" feelings coming over you, see if you can just observe them instead of trying to cover them up. Don't stop achieving things, but do stop looking to your accomplishments to provide you with a sense of identity and worth. Your spouse loves you for who you are, not what you've done.

Now What?

You may have clearly recognized your pattern or shtick among those described. You may even see yourself in several of them. You may have some but not all of the symptoms of a particular pattern. You may have found a pattern that has shown up in some but not all of your previous relationships. Or you may not have found your particular shtick.

Remember, these are common patterns, and common patterns are never exactly like real life. If the description of a pattern doesn't fit you like a glove, don't quibble. If it has any elements that apply to your situation, you will benefit from taking the position that it is a form of sabotage you are practicing. If you can't identify your pattern, then use the examples as models for how to look for your own. Trust me, there are an unlimited number of shticks out there, and some of them are yours.

Maybe you don't see your pattern clearly or understand yet how you are actually sabotaging your relationships. In that case, assuming responsibility will require a leap of faith. But once you're willing to see yourself as a saboteur, the insights about how you do it will dawn on you. There's one thing you can't miss: The common link in every pattern is going to be you.

What if you think you have no pattern? What if you are positive the problem is your spouse, but definitely not you? This may seem like a laudable position to be in, but it's not. Unless you can discover the ways you undermine the marriage, you will not be able to stop doing it. If the problems in your marriage are not caused by you, you cannot correct them.

It's in your own best interest to discover how you sabotage your relationship, so I suggest you go back to the beginning of this chapter and review the material. Then reread the descriptions of the five shticks and see if you can find yours. If you only have part of one, or you feel uncomfortable just reading one, odds are it's yours.

What if you see yourself in every shtick? Don't get nervous, you're not a hopeless case, just a bit overanalytical. Focus on reforming the pattern that gives you the most trouble.

Now that you've identified your shtick or pattern, you can begin to turn it around. But don't expect it to disappear overnight. This behavior is a habit by now, so you will have to exercise discipline in order to stop repeating it.

Before I identified my pattern, I was unaware of my suppressive behavior toward men. Once I knew what to look for, I began to catch myself. At first, just as in the parking lot, I noticed it *after* I did it. With a little more practice, I began to catch myself *while* I was doing it. Eventually, I was able to catch myself *before* I started to behave this way and stop myself. It took discipline just to stick with it at first, but soon the habit diminished in strength.

Remember this: When something is going wrong in your relationship, the trick is to *look* for your pattern. This goes counter to our natural tendency, which is to assume we are not the one at fault. But if you are even willing to consider being the one responsible for the difficulty or disagreement, it will give you power—the power to do something about it. In the heat of the moment, it may seem hard to stand back and take responsibility, but believe me it is less difficult than trying to change your mate.

An added benefit is that when you are willing to take responsibility, it is more likely and easier for your partner to do the same. When someone is not being attacked and not having to defend himself, it is much easier for him to own up to whatever he may have done to contribute to the problem.

The pitfall of this chapter would be to use this information to analyze your partner's pattern rather than your own. Don't go there! Any efforts you make in this direction will be fruitless. The power to enhance and nurture your marriage will only come from self-awareness.

Exercises in Creating What You Want

A. From your observations, what were your mother's negative attitudes and rules about marriage? This doesn't necessarily mean the things she said about marriage (although it could), but rather how she acted. For example, did your mother rely on your father to make financial or political decisions? Was it your mother who took care of all the needs of the children? Look deep for these answers; the more you can uncover, the more power you will have over your own life.

    1.

    2.

    3.

    4.

    5.

B. From your observations, what were your father's negative attitudes and rules about marriage? (For example: Men have to provide for women. Men work harder and should be taken care of by their wives. Women take care of the house and kids. Men's work is more important than women's work.)

    1.

    2.

    3.

4.

5.

C. Describe your own negative attitudes and rules about marriage. (For example: My husband comes first. Men don't know what it takes to have a great marriage. I can't have as many friends as before I was married.)

1.

2.

3.

4.

5.

D. Answer the following questions:

1. What problems or complaints have you had in past relationships or in your present one? Be specific: What didn't work?

1.

2.

3.

4.

5.

2. What *has* worked in your past or present relationships?

1.

2.

3.

4.

5.

3. In your opinion, the trouble with men/women is: (For example: men are babies; women are after

one thing; men are after one thing; men are insensitive; women are too sensitive.)

E. From the above exercises:
    1. Of the negative beliefs and attitudes that you
       have identified, list those that are affecting your
       present relationship.
        1.
        2.
        3.
        4.
        5.

    2. List the positive beliefs and attitudes that are
       currently in place and you want to continue.
        1.
        2.
        3.
        4.
        5.

    3. Now, list new positive beliefs and attitudes that
       you have not had in the past but would like to
       have now.
        1.
        2.
        3.
        4.
        5.

F. Interview at least two happily married couples about
   their relationships. Ask them how they met, their
   first impressions of each other, the ingredients that

make their relationships successful, and so on. Unfortunately, the challenge will be in finding two happily married couples. We're not looking for the longest married, but couples you are moved by or impressed with. Find couples who have been together more than ten years and still openly show love, respect, admiration, and passion for each other.

This is a gold mine to be tapped. Find out everything you can from them. Get every secret. Be specific with your questions. If you just ask them what works in their marriage you probably won't get as much useful information as you would if you asked them how they handle specific issues, such as when they get really bored with each other or truly hated each other's guts. Is it still romantic? In what ways? Be willing to be a little (but politely) intrusive.

G. Write an essay about your "ideal relationship."

List the qualities that are important to you: how you are together, what you do together, how you communicate. Describe these qualities in terms of what you want, *not* in terms of what you don't want. For example, instead of, "He doesn't place a lot of demands on my time," say, "He is respectful of my life and my commitments." Instead of, "She doesn't try to change me," say, "She makes me feel appreciated and adored."

Share the essay with your spouse.

H. Make a relationship collage.

You'll need poster board, glue, scissors, and a pile of magazines. Go through magazines and cut out images and words that illustrate what you want in a relationship. Use the information you wrote in your essay to guide you. Make a collage out of these images and any other items—photographs, drawings, meaningful objects—you would like to include.

People sometimes think this exercise is silly. It's not. It is a different way to get in touch with your vision of what a relationship can be, and it makes your ideal relationship seem less vague and more tangible and attainable. Many of the same people who resist doing this exercise afterward report that they find it moving and inspiring.

No two collages ever look the same. Just use your imagination and creativity—and have fun. When you are finished, show your collage to your spouse and explain to her or him what the images represent to you. You may want to hang it where it can be a source of inspiration for you.

I. What is your shtick?

Name it, describe it, give examples, provide as much detail as you can. Share your shtick with your spouse.

A good resource for this chapter is my book, *How Not to Stay Single*. I've used a great deal of information from it for this chapter. The same negative attitudes and behavior patterns that hinder single people in finding relationships are often carried forward and sabotage the long-term ones.

Watch What You Say

The words we speak don't just describe our reality, they create it.

I love to dance and majored in dance in college. But early in our relationship I made the mistake of telling Tony he was a lousy dancer. Because of my background and Tony's respect for my opinion, my words carried a lot of weight with him. Now I'm married to a guy who is very fit and has great agility and rhythm and thinks he is a lousy dancer. No matter how much I now try to convince him otherwise, I haven't been able to undo the reality I created and stuck myself with years ago just by opening my big mouth. And I'm sure if I knew the consequences of some of the other things I have said to people in my life, I would be even more dismayed.

None of us is sufficiently aware of the power of our words. One simple, thoughtless statement can have far-reaching repercussions. When your words involve another person, your influence not only runs far but deep.

How Do You Speak About Your Spouse?

I often hear married people talk about their relationships in the most disparaging terms, calling one's wife the "ball and chain" or "the warden," as if marriage is the end of life, freedom, fun, happiness, and sex. Given the image married people give marriage, it's not surprising that there are so many forty-year-olds who don't want to commit. It's as though they think commitment means what I thought it meant as a child—that men in white jackets come to take you away.

The way you talk about your spouse and your relationship has a profound impact and makes a lasting impression.

You may think that, as an adult, your partner should be immune to the impact of what you say, but that isn't the case. And unfortunately, the most common pattern of speaking about a spouse is in a demeaning manner. It's almost like bragging: *I can put down my partner, I know him that well. Or, I am so intimate with her that I am entitled to teasingly expose her faults to others.*

If your spouse complains that the teasing is hurtful, you respond that you were "just joking," and "don't be so sensitive."

How often do you hear—or say—"My spouse is stubborn, a spendthrift, stupid about finances, or useless around the house; couldn't care less about the relationship, or sex, or taking care of the children, dogs, car, paying the taxes."

The trouble is, you are taking negative patterns and reinforcing them with these comments. Yes, you might get a few laughs, but are they worth the cost of imprinting unwanted behavior even deeper onto the reputation and self-image of your partner?

I enjoy spending money. I think I do it well and I derive great pleasure from shopping, traveling, and lessons of every kind for myself and my children. I can make jokes about myself this way, and Tony certainly has gotten mileage out of his stories about my sprees.

Then, during one of our tougher times, I was making it a point to be very careful about my spending, yet I continued to be razzed by Tony about being a spendthrift. I got no credit from him for being responsible or for having changed my behavior. When I heard him tease or make the usual sarcastic comments, my thoughts were contradictory, "If he doesn't even notice my efforts, I might as well enjoy myself and 'shop till I drop.' "

Not only are you saying things that are counterproductive to what you want, you are often saying things that hurt (which is also not what you want). You may think your spouse *shouldn't* be hurt by your sarcasm, jokes, and teasing, but she or he is. We all are. No one likes to be belittled, even if it makes for a great laugh. If you want to entertain, tell one on yourself, not one at the expense of the feelings of another.

This is a red flag; check your attitude. If you feel resentment or anger about some of the things you are teasing about, use Chapter 5 to work through it honestly.

Include Yourself

Nothing makes a person more unattractive than low self-esteem. People are most appealing when they are self-fulfilled, passionate, and joyous in their own lives. It is much easier to be turned on and "in love" with a partner who is excited and happy about themselves and all of the things they are up to or involved with.

The lowest point in our marriage was when Tony's self-esteem was suffering. We had moved to Santa Fe from Seattle thinking we had sufficient investments to support ourselves without full-time employment. Tony had been a part owner of his company in Seattle and had always been successful and completely occupied and productive with his work. After a short time in Santa Fe, however, one of our investments in Seattle began to sour. At first we assumed it was a temporary turn in the market, and we didn't respond even as more trouble surfaced. I think by then we had slipped into a state of denial about the severity of the situation. We were living peacefully removed from reality in the "Land of Enchantment" and had become almost complacent about money matters. We had developed a sense of false confidence that we would easily be able to get through the situation. I must admit, I was the greater proponent of this way of thinking and was critical of Tony when he spoke of his concerns.

Tony recognized what was happening much sooner than I did and started looking at business opportunities in Santa Fe. Over the next few years we tried several ventures, all of which failed or produced very little income. While I never lost confidence in or respect for Tony, each failure chipped away at his self-esteem and confidence; he became more and more depressed.

It's very interesting that, although I am the one in the family who is the bigger spender, I adjusted to having less money more easily than Tony did. Although I missed shopping and traveling, my self-worth was not tied to our financial situation, but Tony's was. For him it was a feeling of personal failure as man, husband, and provider for his family.

At first, I did everything I could to bolster Tony in how he felt about our situation and himself. But frankly, after a while, I grew tired of coming home from having a great time with my friends to a depressed husband and trying to make him feel better. Tony wasn't depressed all the time. He would always have fun with the kids and want to play around with me, too. But more and more, whenever we were together, he was preoccupied and worried about our finances.

Eventually, I began to ignore what was going on with Tony. I'd spend my days going on glorious horseback rides with friends and then just hang out with the kids when I was home. I gave up trying to make Tony feel better and just took care of myself and the children. Not surprisingly, this didn't work too well.

Then Tony and I signed up for a course on personal growth and development. Driving to the first session, Tony asked me what I hoped to accomplish in the seminar. The words came out of my mouth without thinking and shocked both of us: "I want to save our marriage."

We had not been fighting, so my declaration was not a reaction to some recent incident. Instead, when I looked for an explanation for my dramatic announcement, I found it was not that we weren't getting along, but rather that the life and vitality of our marriage had disappeared. I told Tony I wasn't thinking about leaving nor was I looking for someone else. But there was no way I was going to accept staying together in a dead relationship. Unless our life together was incredible, it was unacceptable as far as I was concerned. I also knew that I could and would do something to remedy the situation. In fact, that was why we were on our way to the course.

This is a good example of a time where telling the truth about what was wrong was important, even though it was acutely embarrassing for me. As a "relationship expert," it was not easy to admit my own marriage was in trouble. But if I had kept up the pretense that everything was wonderful, when in fact it was not, the marriage truly would have been hopeless and impossible to save. Yes, we might have stayed together, but as I've said before, merely staying together is not my goal.

The course we took certainly got us back on the road to

health. And along the way I learned several important lessons. One of the biggest was how necessary the self-esteem of each partner is to a relationship. It is often said that until you love yourself, you cannot love anyone else. I believe that *unless* you love yourself, you won't let anyone else love you. During this period in our relationship, I realized how hard it was to continue to love someone who hated himself.

One evening, as I was trying to cajole Tony into feeling better, I suddenly felt as I did when I was a new and inexperienced teacher. A whining child would complain to me about having nothing to do. I'd give them an idea, and they'd whine about that. I'd give them another idea, and they'd whine about the new idea. This would go on until I was completely frustrated and angry with the child. Instead of helping the child, I had been manipulated into feeling just as miserable as they were acting. It didn't take me long to learn not to get pulled into that game. Yet here I was feeling the same thing happening with Tony.

So I told Tony that if he was feeling bad, *he* needed to find some way or do something that would make him feel better. I had already learned not to let him take his frustrations out on me, that I was not the enemy. Still, he would sometimes try to turn the situation around in a way that made it look as though I was mad at him for not making money, and, therefore, *I* was the reason he was feeling so much pressure. He was hurting and suffering and wanted to lash out at someone. I knew if I let him get away with attacking me, it would not help either of us.

I told him that it wasn't my job to make him happy. His response was, "It isn't?" (This conversation was a revelation for *both* of us.) I said I was more than willing to do anything to support him, but he was the one who needed to be responsible for his own well-being and happiness. It was at this moment I had a real sense of what it meant to be "co-dependent." And it was not a trap I was going to fall into.

Tony needed to find a job—not just because we needed the money, but because he was happier and felt better about himself when he was engrossed and involved in a business activity. He really loves being engaged in projects and struggling with the details it takes for things to succeed. He's a brilliant business-man, and he's most alive and energized when that is what he is doing. When both of us realized the truth of this, our relation-ship turned around.

But knowing how important it is to value and love yourself doesn't necessarily make it happen. The question is, what do you do to raise your own self-esteem?

For some people, low self-esteem can be a function of deeply rooted, systemic problems that are unlikely to be resolved with-out the help of a skilled therapist. For many others, low self-esteem is due, in large part, to bad habits that can be overcome with some conscious effort and discipline and, most importantly, through altering how you speak about yourself.

Many of us were taught as children that it is not polite to speak highly of ourselves. We got into the habit of minimizing our achievements and magnifying our faults. More attention is paid to our flaws and the things we would like to change than to the things we do well and make us feel good. And as I said in the last chapter, putting attention on something—whatever it may be—strengthens and reinforces it.

Recognizing your own worth and value is not the same as being conceited. And putting yourself down is not the same as being humble and modest.

Do you constantly make negative pronouncements, such as "I have no discipline," "I'm too indecisive," "I'll never be success-ful," or "I can't get organized"? When you make a mistake, do you say, "I'm so dumb," "I have the worst memory," "I'm just insensitive," or some other habitual self-deprecation?

Okay, so you're not perfect. But must you keep dwelling on

your imperfections? Even if you don't voice these insecurities, your internal dialogue reinforces them and creates a sense of low self-esteem that comes across to others. If you had a friend who was as critical of you as you are of yourself, you would have broken off the friendship long ago. You already know it doesn't work to be with a partner who constantly points out *your* short-comings, yet that's what you do to yourself. Cut it out!

Instead of empowering your faults by constantly focusing on them, emphasize your strengths. This will not only give you more confidence, it will validate the fact that your spouse made a great choice and is fortunate to be with you.

Home Is Where Your Garbage Can Is

You have had a long, grueling day at work where you had to keep up a nonstop good front for the boss and customers. You had to take it all with patience and understanding. Your boss, in particular, aimed his frustrations directly at you, and now you can't stand him or anyone else who ever walked through the office door. Finally, you come home where you can let all your own frustrations out. You can be rude, short, or not communicate at all. You can even be angry and your spouse will love you and understand. You can act like a slob and look like one, too, because you're home. You can be at your worst at home, because you had to be at your best at work.

I know your spouse is supposed to be someone to whom you can pour out all of your problems, insecurities, and frustrations. Someone who will allow you to be your worst, with whom you can let it all hang out. Someone who will stick with you rich or poor, fat or thin. Someone who will love you no matter what.

But we take advantage of the love and understanding we are given. We keep raising the ante, testing how much someone will put up with before they leave. You mistake your spouse for a landfill. Few relationships can survive, let alone flourish, under the weight of the garbage we dump on them. Testing the stability or strength of a relationship is a mistake, if only because divorce is so readily available today.

Marriages are fragile and precious, and in order to last and flourish they need to be treated as such. Just as you know children are sensitive and impressionable, and it is wrong to take your feelings of frustration out on them, the same is true of your marriage. Your spouse is someone you cherish and love. He or she is undoubtedly one of the most important people in your life. You need to be your best, look your best, and give your best to this person.

So, if you can't let down with your spouse, what do you do, kick the dog? No, and for the same reason you shouldn't take your feelings out on your loved ones—because it doesn't work. It won't make you feel any better. You may feel less anger after you kick the dog, but now you feel guilty and horrible for inflicting pain. And guilt is often worse than the feelings of anger and frustration.

The answer is to *share* your feelings with your spouse. Share your day and everything that troubled or frustrated you. You may come home angry and not want to talk to anyone about anything, but you need to release these feelings. Opening up to your partner will not only eliminate the tension and stress, it will also deepen the intimacy of the marriage.

If you are really steamed up, tell your partner you are going to go do something physically strenuous for thirty minutes and *then* you'd like to talk about your day. Or if you must rant and rave, ask your spouse *first* if he or she would be willing to let you express yourself with some volume. But honor your spouse and your relationship by refusing to use them as a dumping ground.

The Midas Mouth

Remember the story of King Midas, who was granted his wish that everything he touched would turn to gold? If he had known beforehand what that would mean, he would have made a different wish.

In the same way, if you knew that what you said about your marriage would be what you ended up having, you would probably make some changes in what you say. Well, it's true; what you say is what you get.

This has been proven to me consistently, time after time. In my seminars for singles, I always talk glowingly about Tony. I tell them how funny he is, how handsome, thoughtful, and how he is such a great father. I emphasize his positive qualities because I want to inspire people. I want them to see that not only can they find a relationship, but an incredible one as well. They don't have to settle for something less than great. So I'll be in Dallas talking about Tony at home in Santa Fe, telling the group all the details of how wonderful he is—and I find myself gushing with love for him.

This "gushiness" carries over into my everyday conversations, and people are always surprised that Tony and I are not newlyweds. Their reaction always makes me wonder: Aren't relationships *supposed* to get better over time? Why are they so surprised?

As I said in the introduction, in the process of gathering information about what makes a great relationship, I have studied many other couples, especially those I thought had loving and extraordinary marriages. I looked for qualities I admired and wanted for myself. In doing this, I realized how I qualified these couples as role-model relationships was a direct result of how they *talked* about their marriage and spouse.

I remember talking to Sylvia about how inspired I was by her marriage to Zollie. He is always telling people about Sylvia, about what an interesting, adventurous, loving person she is. If I tell Zollie something funny, he'll ask me if I told Sylvia, that she'd love to know. Or he rushes over to tell her himself. Sylvia told me Zollie is always that way with her. "What you see, is how he is. He's always been attentive, loving, and admiring." She always feels adored and appreciated. (They had been married *fifty years* at the time of this conversation.)

Now I don't know what they're like when they're alone—that would be impossible. The only thing I know is how they speak about each other. Unfortunately, it is an exception to hear couples speak about each other in the positive way of Zollie and Sylvia.

When you speak well of each other it stands out. It is unusual, and your love and admiration touch everyone within hearing distance. Conversely, when you speak poorly of your spouse, it damages not only how others think of your marriage, but how the two of you think of it as well.

Karen and Bill took my seminar. They had been married ten years and, if you asked them, they thought they had a good marriage. If you asked their friends, however, you got a different story. People were jolted by the way he reprimanded her, criticized her, and ordered her around. It made it very uncomfortable to be with them.

Usually she would let the way he talked to her slide off her back. She knew he loved her and didn't mean the horrible things he said. But sometimes it would be too much to bear and overwhelm her. She came to me after one of these browbeating sessions to ask for advice. She was afraid this time he meant what he said and was going to leave her.

I told Karen if she wanted to save her marriage, she needed to stop tolerating Bill's behavior. She needed to put a stop to it immediately. It was up to her not to let Bill say these things. By letting them go by, she was actually compounding the problem. Karen had thought that letting Bill vent his anger, at her expense, was doing him a service, that she was being a good and understanding wife. She was wrong.

Verbal abuse, like physical abuse, hurts the perpetrator as much, if not more, than the victim. People hate themselves when they've caused pain to someone, especially someone they love. The person they have abused is a reminder of what they did and, therefore, of how disgusted they are with themselves for having done it. They then resent their victim for making them feel that way.

What woke Karen up was hearing that, without exception, everyone who had met or who knew her and Bill commented on his behavior toward her. She turned white when she heard this. Karen had gotten so used to Bill's behavior that she was oblivious to the impression it made on others. Now she realized how horrible they, and especially Bill, must have looked to their friends.

Deep down, she knew he loved her and cared for her, and in one sense it didn't make a difference what others thought. But in another, more fundamental sense, it did matter. She loved her husband, knew his great qualities, and was very proud of him, so it horrified her that anyone would ever think poorly of him. The best part of this revelation was that she clearly saw *she* was the one who could turn the situation around.

What surprised her was Bill's change in behavior when she no longer allowed him to verbally attack her. She had been afraid he would become violent if she cut off his tirades. Instead, he became more loving, appreciative, and respectful. The turnaround for them was visibly noticeable to others. A mutual friend remarked to me how supportive Bill was at a talk Karen gave—standing in the back as proud as can be, bragging about her to others.

The Power Is on the Tip of Your Tongue

Nothing is more gratifying and romantic than to hear your spouse tell someone how wonderful you are. Never do you feel more loved. At the same time, it regenerates the love in the one who is speaking.

This is a discipline and practice I have taken to heart, because I have found that my speaking about Tony creates the person I get to live with. If all I point out are his weaknesses, mistakes, or faults—or if I decide some things are character flaws rather than just mistakes—then that becomes my reality, my experience, of the person I have chosen to be with. If I find myself living with someone I don't like, it doesn't say much for me, nor will it be nurturing to us or to our children.

You have a choice about how you speak and what you say. So you might as well choose to say something that will empower your spouse—and therefore your relationship. This doesn't mean you have to make up things or lie. At first, you may have to look harder for complimentary attributes because you are used to being negative. It may require some discipline to break your old habits. And you might not look so "hip" extolling your spouse's virtues. You may even have to risk looking corny.

Just remember: You are not choosing what you say as much as you are choosing how your marriage will be. Whether you have an extraordinary relationship is up to you.

You *Make the Call*

There is a story about three umpires discussing the game of baseball and the art of calling a pitch either a strike or a ball. The rookie umpire said, "I call it the way it is." The more seasoned umpire said, "I call it the way I see it." At which point the veteran umpire spoke up, "It ain't nothin' until I call it."

It's up to you to call your relationship the way you want it to be—and then the way you want it to be will be the way it is!

Exercises in Creating What You Want

A. This week, tell one person a day about your spouse. Brag about how great she or he is. At least two of these times, do this while your spouse is present.

B. Tell one person a day about how great your marriage is. Say what you love about being married and especially what you love about being married to your partner. Then tell your spouse these same things.

Talk the Talk

If you ask a real estate broker for the three most important elements of a successful property, the reply will be "Location, location, location." If you ask me for the three most important elements of a successful, long-term relationship, my reply will be "Communication, communication, communication."

Communication is the medium through which relationships are created and in which they continue to exist. Communication is as essential to the survival of a relationship as oxygen is to the body. If you were to compare the maintenance of your relationship to that of your body, then regular communication—by which I mean *talking* and *listening* to each other—is the equivalent of the aerobic portion of your workout.

Relationships are intangible, they only exist in the space between two people—space that is connected by communication. Most people think they hold their relationships, like their love, somewhere inside themselves. What is "inside," however, is only a history or collection of memories. Relationships, like love, must be expressed to exist. To keep love—and relationships—alive, you must talk.

Communication is the foundation for the health and strength of a marriage. A common reaction, when relationships start to lose their luster, is to think that somehow you misjudged and picked the wrong partner. Just as nothing in the universe is capable of sustaining perpetual motion, there is no such thing as a self-generating, self-maintaining relationship. Any relationship, even the match made in heaven or the union of "soul mates," will gradually begin to drift, grow apart, wither, and die without ongoing and substantial doses of communication.

And I'm not just talking about "quality time." Here quantity counts—the actual amount of time you spend *each* day talking to each other. The more you talk, the more intimate you will be. This is the surefire, foolproof guarantee against growing apart.

The amount of time an average couple spends talking to each other in a day is *less than four minutes!* This includes "Pass the salt" and "Who's picking up the dry cleaning?" No wonder so many married people feel alone. I'm sure this also explains why so many divorces are justified with the comment "We just grew apart."

Just as neglecting your workout results in getting out of shape, the less you talk to each other, the less you will have to say. The reverse is also true: The more you talk, the more you will have to say to each other. Trust me, you are not going to run out of things to say. You haven't run out of things to say to the friends or business associates you see every day, have you?

You often hear that for a marriage to work you have to do things together, have shared interests, or shared goals. Nah! You don't need to do everything together, but you do need to relate to each other your experience of what you do. You need time to be together and talk about your individual or shared interests, your feelings, goals, and dreams.

I love to ride horses, but Tony does not share my passion. He loves to play tennis, a sport for which I have no interest (or skill). But I get a thrill listening to him talk about how he finally beat someone he has played with for two years. I love it when Tony is turned on and sharing his passion with me. And he is just as interested and supportive when I tell him about an unbelievable ride I had.

I don't mean that doing things together isn't wonderful, it's just that it isn't necessary to a close and vibrant partnership. Only one thing is absolutely necessary: talking to each other.

So Tell Me Something I Don't Know!

Everyone already knows how important communication is in a marriage. As you started reading this chapter you probably said to yourself, "Yes, yes, I know it's important. My wife has been telling me that for years!" If I asked the "couch potato" who hasn't said anything to his wife since the honeymoon except "Honey, get me a beer!" whether he thought it was important to talk with his wife every now and then, I'm sure *he* would agree. It might take some time for him to get focused on the question, but if the question is, "Do I think communication is important in a good marriage?" then the answer is, "Yes, of course it is."

Some of us will try to fool ourselves into believing we have this communication thing handled. "Oh, she knows how I feel," he might say to the marriage counselor when asked if he loved his wife. "After all, I married her, didn't I?"

Tony admits to being guilty of this in his first marriage. He has told me, "I knew we weren't talking enough, and that she wasn't happy. I just didn't want to face it or take responsibility for it. 'Things are fine,' I would say to myself as I headed for the golf course. But in my heart I knew they weren't."

Knowing that communication works and doing it are often two different things. You need to find ways to recognize when you are in a rut or fall into a pattern of "not communicating." And you need to know how to get out of ruts and break those patterns to avoid the breakdowns that will be yours to deal with if you don't.

This chapter will get you started and deal with the basics of communication. The next four chapters will give you some additional help in working through the most common pitfalls and hazards in communication.

One Hour a Day, Just Do It

The most important homework assignment I give in my workshops is to talk to your partner for one hour a day *every day.* At first, I hear nothing but complaints: "I don't have an hour." "We're not home at the same times." "I can't get him to talk for five minutes, let alone an hour." "We can't do that, we have kids!" "We could never think of enough things to say to fill a whole hour." (Have I included your excuse?)

Everyone has reasons—valid reasons—why taking the time to do this exercise is not practical. I understand how hectic people's lives are, and I would never waste an hour of your time needlessly. I give this assignment because it really works and is necessary to the health and longevity of your relationship. If you aren't willing to do it, I'd suggest you look again at how serious you are about having a good and lasting relationship.

Remember, I am the person who thinks relationships don't

take *work*, but I do think they take *time*. Those of us who work out regularly *make* the time to jog or lift weights, and we do it because our physical health is a priority. Is the health and growth of your marriage a priority? How important is it to you that this relationship not end up dead or in divorce court? If you answered these questions positively and honestly, you will make the time to have these daily conversations.

The biggest priority in my life is my marriage. It is the foundation and support for everything. Of course, I consider my children my biggest responsibility, but I know the greatest gift I can give them is a stable, loving, respectful marriage. It is obvious the sense of security this provides for them. But also, even though my children are quite young, I can already see the benefits of their having parents who show love and respect for each other.

Being married has made me more effective in every area of my life than I ever was before. First of all, before I met Tony, no matter what I was doing, a part of me was looking to connect with a man. Having a foundation of love and support from which I can draw gives me added power to put into any activity I pursue. I am able to focus 100 percent on whatever I do, whether it is reading to my children or writing a book.

All this for the minor investment of an hour a day. So get up an hour earlier, or stay up an hour later. Meet for lunch. Talk while you jog together, or if one of you is on the road, use the phone. But do it.

OK, I'll Do It, but What If My Spouse Won't?

How do you get an uncooperative or uncommunicative partner to participate? I had this very issue with Tony. If you asked him what was the best part of our relationship, what meant the most, he would tell you talking to each other, being close and not alone. Even so, Tony often resists talking. He'll come home from work, and I'll ask him:

> "How was your day?"
> "Fine."
> "Anything interesting happen at work?"
> "No.
> "What did you work on?"
> "Same old stuff."

By this time, Tony is showing signs of irritation and itching to get rid of me so he can be alone with the newspaper. I used to respond to this with hurt and fury. I'd want to give up, call a girlfriend so I could have someone to talk to, or just go off by myself and eat a bag of cookies. But whenever I did get him going and we were engaged in conversation, Tony was great and totally into it. He is a great conversationalist; he's smart, fascinating, and very funny. So I had to figure out a way that was guaranteed to ease him into the routine.

What I discovered worked was to warm him up or "prime the pump." I'd start with the same, "How was your day?" Then I would move into more specific questions that required more than a "yes" or "no" answer. "Which deal did you work on today?" "What was the response to the e-mail you sent yesterday?" "Did you see or talk to anyone I know or am interested in?" "What do you want to accomplish in your meeting tomorrow?" This warm-up phase is not my favorite thing to do in our relationship, but it works. Tony eventually opens up and we really talk (and from this conversation I get information for follow-up questions during warm-up the next day).

Most important, it's worth it. We are closer; we are real partners in our life together. We each have someone who knows and cares about us, and neither of us feels alone even when we're apart. In fact, I find that when I am away and something wonderful happens, the first thing that occurs to me is to tell Tony.

Do I get upset that I am always the one who has to do the work to get the conversation going? No, it's not worth getting troubled over. I do it because it is natural for me, and I'm better at it. Tony is better at handling the bills and wrestling with the kids. But the main reason I do it is because it works. And out of this, I have an incredible relationship.

Over the years we have been doing this, Tony has developed great communication skills. So when I don't feel like talking, he knows what to do to get *me* to open up. Many times he is the one to detect we need more time alone to talk, and he initiates our conversations. It is important to understand that if Tony didn't do this early in our relationship it was not because he didn't want to, but because he didn't have the skills.

Feedback from couples who do this homework shows the results are nothing short of miraculous. As a result of doing the hour-long conversations, people report they have the kind of relationship they always envied in others and only dreamed of for themselves. For many, this happens after only *one week* of the homework.

By the second week, the moans about how difficult it is to fit these talks into schedules have disappeared. Instead, I hear stories about their extraordinary efforts to schedule talk time. Husbands call from airports or directly from the airplane; wives call from car phones between appointments, interrupting husbands in business meetings to schedule their talk for the day. When the benefits are so real, communication quickly becomes a priority.

Inevitably, there are one or two couples in each course who don't do the homework the first week. They soon realize they are the unlucky ones and are envious of the results they hear from other couples. The sharing from the "doers" always convinces those who didn't get the job done to get on board.

Sid and Lynn had been married for fifteen years and had three children. Their schedules were crazy with both of them working full-time and sharing the care of the kids. Between meals, piano lessons, homework, and soccer games, they saw each other a lot but weren't talking about much more than working out their weekly routine. They knew they cared for one another but, in truth, they were existing on memories of how they used to be. They took the course because they were so impressed by friends who had taken it and suddenly became romantic and close. Sid and Lynn wanted that for themselves.

When I assigned the homework the first week, their moans were the loudest. They simply did not have the time. When I suggested one hour less sleep, they couldn't agree upon a time that worked for both of them. Sid was an early morning person, and Lynn was a night owl. So I had them negotiate. The solution they came up with was to have their talks from 5:30 to 6:30 A.M. for one week and from 11:30 P.M. to 12:30 A.M. the next week. Was it easy? No. Was it worth it? You bet it was.

First of all, once they got going, the talks often lasted more than an hour. Many mornings the kids woke up to their parents engrossed in conversations in which they joined or at least were interested in listening to. At night, Sid and Lynn ended up getting less sleep, but, overall, they felt more loved, secure, and relaxed—which ultimately was more refreshing and more nourishing than that extra hour of sleep.

In addition, a lot more sex was happening—an added benefit. Sex is a natural outflow of communication. But I'll talk more about sex in a later chapter.

Listening

Do you sometimes pretend to be listening while glancing at the newspaper on the other side of the table, trying to read the article upside down? Or do you listen to the television news in the background as your spouse tells you what his or her day was like? Well, stop it! Learn to discipline yourself into always giving full attention to your spouse. Anything less is demeaning and insulting.

I told my friend Lisa I was writing this book, and I asked her what it was about Karl that made him a great husband. Her eyes lit up and, without hesitation, she said, "He always takes time to listen to me." Her response was easy for me to relate to, because I have the same experience with Karl. When you are in a conversation with him, you really feel he is interested in what you have to say. Now, Karl is a psychiatrist, so I expect his ability to listen to people is a quality he has developed. Still, it is notable that his wife feels his ability to listen is the one paramount thing that she would use to describe why he is a great husband.

I like the analogy of it as well—that is, if you want to be a *great* spouse, listen to your partner as if listening was your job, as if *all* of what he or she has to say is important and has significance. Listen with interest and even enthusiasm!

How often do we treat our spouse to that kind of attentiveness? For many of us it's difficult. We have busy lives, we're preoccupied with our jobs, our finances, the kids, ourselves. But just because it's hard is not an excuse for giving your partner only "left over" attention.

Yogi Berra, the legendary baseball player who has a way with words, once said, "You can observe a lot just by watching." Well, you can hear a lot just by listening. If the only improvement you made in the area of "communication" was to start listening to your spouse more carefully and with more involvement, you would see remarkable changes in your relationship.

To really listen to your partner is a gift of love that is far more significant than, say, remembering Valentine's Day. I'm not suggesting that forgetting special occasions is advisable, I'm just trying to put it into perspective. If you want to demonstrate, on a regular basis, the love and respect you have for your spouse, then make the effort to listen!

What You "Already Know" Is Stunting Your Spouse's Growth

Time together breeds familiarity, and we all seem to take pride in "knowing" our spouse better than anyone else. "My wife will love that movie." "I know my husband, he'd never go to the opera." You can think of many examples of what you *know* he or she wouldn't do.

What "knowing" tends to unwittingly do is create a static shell around that person, a shell that not only freezes them in place the way they are but makes change very difficult.

My father was a "meat and potatoes" man. Even though the rest of the family liked Chinese food, we only ate it when Dad was out of town. After my mother died, my father started to eat Chinese food, and do many other things he "didn't do."

My mother hadn't made my father stay "the way he was." Instead, he became trapped by her expectations, by what she already knew about him—which he had originally set up himself. There is a tendency to become molded by and then stay the way others expect us to be. If we change, we not only shock our partner, it may also feel threatening to the relationship. The threat, however, comes from the feeling of no longer "knowing" who we are living with.

It gets worse. Not only do we "know" how our spouse is, and what they like or don't like, but we also know in advance what they're going to say. *He* may mention that he saw a friend who just got back from Paris and *she* "knows" this is leading to why they should book a vacation they can't afford. She starts to say something about the kids' school and he "knows" they are about to have the public school versus private school argument. The same fight they've had a million times begins before the sentence is even complete. Not only do we "know" in advance what our partner is going to say, we use our "knowledge" to justify not listening. The possibility for a new conversation, a new idea, or a change of opinion is cut off.

This is what causes relationships to feel suppressive. And what gets suppressed is growth, change, newness, and possibility. Of course, it's not intentional. No one would ever want to be accused of such behavior. It is a natural tendency, however, to become accustomed or comfortable with your own interpretation of how your spouse will act or behave. Still, it's dangerous to fall into this pattern, and *you should be on guard at all times against thinking or acting as if you "know" everything about your partner.*

Why? Because most people who have affairs do so for the conversation. The person who wanders is not usually looking for sex as much as they are looking for someone who will listen to them, someone who pays attention and doesn't already know what is going to be said. Sex follows because, as I said earlier, it is a natural (though not necessarily inevitable) outflow of great communication.

Do *you* have the same opinions, tastes, and interests you had when you were twenty? Of course not. So why shouldn't your spouse continue to change at thirty, forty, fifty, or sixty? Instead of being proud you know your spouse so well, try being open to what you *don't* know. Instead of listening for what you expect he or she will say or think, look for something you hadn't noticed before. It will be exciting for you to learn about these new thoughts, ideas, and interests.

When someone asks me if Tony likes a particular kind of movie, or a certain kind of book, I say, "I don't know. Ask Tony." With this answer I risk them thinking, "She must not be very close to her husband if she doesn't know such simple things about him." But I would rather risk that opinion than in any way be a party to suppressing Tony's growth and development.

How Not *to Get What You Want*

Answer: *complain!*

For something that doesn't work, it's amazing how much time we spend complaining about the inconveniences and issues in our relationships.

Communicating through complaints is immature. It is a childish way of attempting to accomplish change. Yet we do it because we are creatures of habit, and at some point in our lives, usually when we were children, we learned that complaining worked. "I'm hungry!" you said to your mother, and you got fed. "I hurt myself!" you cried, and your mother gave you comfort. As a child, you weren't expected to be more specific and say "I'm hungry, will you please fix me a snack?" The desired result just appeared in response to your cries.

But your wife (or husband) is not your mother. And you are not a child. It's time to break the habit of whining as a way of getting what you want.

Let me demonstrate. Let's say I am annoyed that Tony doesn't help with driving our kids to their activities. So I complain to him that he never helps. His response will most likely be defensive. "I do, too! Whenever you travel I drive them everywhere!" Or, "I can't help it if I have to work." Or, he might go on the offense with, "Well, you don't work as hard as I do!" or "When you drive you're always late."

Either type of response to my complaint could easily lead to a much longer, more heated, hurtful, and certainly argumentative conversation. What it rarely leads to is a result anywhere close to what I want.

Turn Your Complaints into Requests

If I want something to happen, the most effective way to get it done is not to complain but to make a request. "Tony, would you drive the kids to school on Friday mornings?"

Now it becomes easy. First of all, Tony is much more willing to help me when he doesn't feel he is being attacked. Second, Tony likes me (a very important and often forgotten assumption in relationships) and, of course, will go out of his way to lend me a hand when he can.

His answer is either yes, no, or something that indicates a willingness to negotiate another solution. For instance, he may say, "I can't do it this Friday, but any Friday I don't have an early staff meeting, I'd love to do it."

Turning complaints into requests tends to save a lot of time, energy, and hurt feelings. More important, it works. You won't get what you want 100 percent of the time, but I guarantee your percentage will go up. Also, the process will be much cleaner and more pleasant.

Some complaints can't be turned into requests—"I hate this rainy weather, and I want it to stop!"—yet they can be used to show you sympathize with a situation that is beyond anyone's control. But almost all the serious complaints you have can be converted to requests. (This tool is not limited to spouses; it also can work like magic with children or anyone else in your life.) And it works with complaints directed at you. A sure way to stop an attack is to ask if the person attacking you has a request.

When I was a teacher, parents and kids often came at me with their complaints. Defending myself was very stressful, tiresome, and unsatisfying. Attacking back was even worse. Asking the complainer if they had a request was the ticket. A parent would say they were unhappy with their child's progress, or they didn't understand what I was covering in class, or they disapproved of some aspect of the school. I'd then ask them if they had a request. The reactions were amusing. Sometimes it stopped them in their tracks. They had been prepared for a battle and just wanted to spout off, so they might come back with, "Well, I just wanted you to know." My response, "Thank you, and please feel free to let me know if you have a specific request."

Or sometimes they would come back with a legitimate request we could work on until we agreed on a course of action. These complaints—now requests—often generated great new ideas.

As I said, this works like magic. The only hard part is not initially reacting to the complaint with a quick defensive or offensive response. But with practice you will find yourself making requests and negotiating your way through conversations that before would have erupted into major battles.

Try a Little Alchemy, Like Turning Straw into Gold

In my relationship classes, each person is asked to come up with a real complaint they have in their marriage and then express that complaint to their partner. I instruct the receiving partner to just notice their reactions but not to respond. Then, I have the "complainer" turn the complaint they just delivered into a request. This is then followed by the two of them working with the request until they reach a satisfactory resolution.

Examples of complaints:

- You watch too much TV.
- You don't call when you're going to be late.
- You spend too much money.
- We don't have sex often enough.

Turned into requests:

- Would you limit watching TV to one hour a night?
- When you're going to be more than thirty minutes late, will you call me?
- Can we agree on a budget?
- Will you "fool around" with me tonight?

At this point, someone always says, "I shouldn't have to make requests for common, considerate behavior. They should *know* to be quiet if I'm still sleeping." Well, maybe they should, but they don't.

One of the worst ailments of marriage is the notion that if they love you, they can read your mind (like your mother did). You can either wait around for this to happen, or you can start getting what you want by asking for it. Personally, I prefer getting what I want.

My favorite request example is with Tony. Tony was concerned about our finances. Goodness knows he had tried the complaint route to curb my shopping but to no avail. At dinner one evening, using the most proper "request" protocol, he politely asked that before I make a purchase of more than $100 would I please consult with him. My quick and very certain response was, "I would divorce you in a second before I would agree to that."

Now, Tony is a shrewd negotiator with a very winning attitude—he always ends up with a yes response. "Well," he countered, "how about every time you spend more than $10,000?" He got his yes. And I got the message.

Get Real

This leads us to the point of making honest requests and getting honest, realistic responses. If someone is chronically late and you request that they be on time and they say yes, most likely this will not end happily.

Don't make ridiculous requests, make workable ones. Of a chronically late spouse you might ask, "Will you call if you're late?" or "Would you be willing to leave fifteen minutes earlier to go to the airport?" and so on.

Also, if someone carelessly says yes to something you don't think will happen, don't accept it. Keep prodding to get more certainty that they *can* and are willing to honor their promise.

This isn't foolproof and you will need some practice at it, but I promise the more you discipline yourself to speak to your partner with requests—never with complaints—the more effective you will be at getting what you want and the more harmonious your relationship will be. In summary, complaining never works, especially in relationships. I think I need to say that again. Complaining to your spouse, about anything, *never, never, never* works. It will not get you the results you want.

Telling the Truth

Solid and lasting partnerships are founded on integrity—a commitment from both persons *always* to be fully open and honest in *all* your communications. I believe this should be a senior promise added to the standard marriage vows, right after "love" and "cherish."

This means being willing to express your own feelings as well as being there to listen to the feelings your spouse expresses. The damage caused by withdrawing and not expressing your feelings is much greater than whatever it is you are feeling and then suppressing. For example, the damage from suppressing the anger you may feel toward your wife for whatever reason is by far more harmful to your relationship than the risk of hurt that might result if you told her how you felt.

Not telling her how you feel undermines the integrity, the foundation of your relationship. But most people stop themselves from communicating because they are fearful of creating "more trouble."

Let's say you just had a talk with your husband and he communicated something that was bothering him. Your job, as noted earlier in this chapter, was simply to listen. You did that, and it really went well—for him. But as he was telling you how unappreciated he feels, you had a bubbling of fire inside. "After all I've done to show my love, he tells me he's unappreciated! I can't believe it!" you think to yourself. But you don't want to say this. If you do, you "know in your heart," you will undermine what you have been trying to accomplish.

So what do you do? Most of us suppress it. We are unwilling to say exactly how we feel. We cool off and the feelings of anger disappear. So it seems that not communicating how we "feel" works better than spilling our guts every time we are upset, or sad, or sorry, or whatever.

It may seem that way, but it's not true. Holding back the communication of your feelings in any relationship, especially a marital one, is damaging. Maybe not in an obvious way, but it's real. When feelings are suppressed, relationships go sour. When you stop saying you are hurt or sad is also when you will stop expressing your love, and when that happens you will lose the passion in your marriage.

You have to be willing to take a few chances in your relationships. If you are angry, you need to find a way to express it. If you are sad, let that be expressed as well. If you stop being willing to express your feelings to your spouse, you will lose the relationship and become two ships passing in the night. (Reread Chapter 4 on communicating strong feelings without dumping them on your partner.)

In the example above, where your husband has just communicated all the things going on with him and it triggered "anger" inside of you, think of a way you could tell him that you felt anger at what he said. You can't just react, you have to find a way to communicate as the author and owner of your feelings, not the victim of his. See if you can separate your anger from yourself enough so that you can talk about it.

When you communicate to your husband about the "anger" you experienced, do so with a sense of responsibility. *He* did not make you angry; it was just a feeling that arose. So communicate it to him in that tone. "I noticed that when you were telling me how you felt, I felt angry." Work on developing your skills at communicating your feelings without blaming each other for them.

The Things You Don't Say

The hidden killers of relationships are often not the things you say but the things you don't say. Most of us have a control problem when it comes to self-expression. Unfortunately, the only regulator we were given was an "on-off" switch. We cannot turn the expression switch on and edit out the things we don't want to come through. What happens when we start to edit is that the switch turns itself off and the self-expression stops.

This does not mean you have to pour out to your partner every thought that comes through your head—*please* spare all of us that interpretation!!! What it does mean is that if you are intentionally, for any reason, holding something back—"He doesn't need to know," "It will hurt her unnecessarily," "It's stupid"—then your love also gets held back.

Like a lie, these withheld communications need more and more camouflage to maintain the cover-up. So even if it wasn't a big deal when it began, it becomes one with time.

Often, when the communication is finally delivered, it's a relief to both parties, especially if it was something silly. But even if it's serious, it's much easier to deal with when it's out in the open.

The important thing to remember here is that you are not the exception, even though you think you can hold back this one thing and it won't hurt. Believe me, you will not get away with it. Personally, I hate that this is true. But it is. And your relationship is not worth the risk.

I took the kids shopping one afternoon. We spent too much money, and I said, "Daddy's going to blow his top when he sees these packages." My son suggested we sneak the packages in and not tell him. I must admit, I considered this solution for a minute, but my response was, "No, I refuse to sneak around or lie to your father. I need to be up front and honest with him just like you guys need to be with me."

Our children are adopted, but they look amazingly like Tony and me. When they were quite young we met a couple who were astounded by the likeness. The man said, "Your children look so much like you, you don't have to tell them they're adopted." I was taken aback by his comment, as if it is shameful to be adopted. But I told him as politely as I could that, first of all, they already knew they were adopted, and second, why would I threaten the foundations of my relationship with them by lying at the very beginning. I would be setting up a future loss of trust that would inevitably occur.

I'm convinced that honesty and integrity make up the core of any good relationship. Withholding, just like lying, weakens the stability of a relationship's foundation. And it usually adds the nagging feeling that something is going on we don't know about. We have all experienced this, the sense that someone is not telling us something, and our reaction is usually to think the worst.

"But if I tell him about the affair he'll leave me."

Yes, he might, but if you don't, the relationship is over anyway. It's like putting poison in the ground, covering it with some dirt, and then expecting your garden to continue to flourish. Eventually, it *will* die!

At least by telling the truth you have a chance to clean up the poison. The process may be incredibly difficult and painful, but if you get through it your relationship will be deeper, stronger, and, most important, still alive.

Exercises in Creating What You Want

The homework in this chapter is the most important homework you can do for the health of your relationship. The bad news is that you need to do it forever. The good news is that if you do it you will always have at your fingertips the tools to have your marriage continue to unfold, blossom, and thrive.

A. Have a one-hour talk with your spouse every day for
   a week—even if you have to do this early in the

morning or late at night. The only guideline is to talk and listen. If you disagree with something he or she says, just notice it and keep listening. Do not argue! You can argue after the hour is over.

B. Each day this week, learn something new about your spouse. Write it down and report your "findings" to each other at the end of the week.
    1.
    2.
    3.
    4.
    5.
    6.
    7.

C. During one of your one-hour talks, list complaints you have with each other. Turn each complaint into a request. Remember, do not respond to the complaint until it is turned into a *request*. (Even if you get upset at the complaint, wait until it is a request, then respond.) Go for closure to each request—be it yes, no, or a counteroffer. After this one session, cut out the complaints altogether. From now on, always start with a request. Abolish complaining from your marriage!

D. Make a list of all the communications you have withheld or not delivered. If something comes to mind, write it down, *all of it*. Do not edit in your head or on the paper. Go back as far as you've known each other and be thorough.

Set up a time to read and listen to each other's lists. Make this time together as private and safe as you can. Remember to be sensitive and caring of each other. Don't interrupt, wait until both of you have read your lists to respond.

Remember that the purpose of this exercise is not to get at each other, it is to clean things up in order to have a more healthy, loving relationship.

If you get into trouble, the information about arguing and forgiveness in Chapter 6 should be helpful.

Fight the
Good Fight

There's no way around it: Couples fight. That in itself is not necessarily a bad thing. Any healthy, long-term relationship has to include the ability to effectively deal with and resolve conflict.

Some people think fighting is one of the healthiest things they have going in their relationship. For these couples, arguments are an acceptable, lively form of self-expression. They say their fights help them clear the air, lead to new levels of understanding, and even add spice and passion to the relationship. If they were not allowed to express themselves in this way, they would feel stifled and cut off in their communication with each other. They sincerely believe that couples who don't fight don't have a good relationship.

Then there are people who are terrified of fighting and think it is damaging to both the individuals and the relationship. Because of their past experience or what they have witnessed, they want to avoid quarrels and the possibility of saying something that can't be taken back. They will do almost anything *not* to fight and believe couples who do fight don't have a good relationship.

Whichever camp you are in, there are serious penalties for foul play when the inevitable disagreements arise. It makes a difference to have a set of rules to follow so that fighting is productive rather than destructive. The six rules below are ones I have developed from my own experience and from working with the couples in my courses. These rules may not help you avoid disagreements, but they will help you fight fair and protect your relationship from unnecessary damage. Because the truth of the matter is that in the heat of the moment, no matter how much we may feel justified, we all need to know when we are hitting below the belt.

Rule #1: You're on the Same Side

This is the golden rule of marital fighting. You cannot afford to forget that your spouse loves you and wants you to have what you want. Remember? That is the basis for your relationship. If you can remember this, then when your partner does something really dreadful, you can see it as a *mistake* rather than as something they are intentionally doing to hurt or anger you.

I was wandering around a multilevel parking lot frantically looking for my car. Tony told me it was on Level D. But it *wasn't* on Level D, or Level C, or Level E for that matter. There I was, in three-inch heels, dressed in a fancy business suit, sweating, late for an important meeting, and racing up and down the ramps. By the time I found the car on Level B, my feet were blistered, I was dripping wet, totally flustered, and ready to kill Tony.

I was too angry to wait until later, so I called him on the car phone, "Do you know what you did? You said it was on D, and now I'm late, I look awful, and my feet are killing me! I can't believe you did this to me!!!"

Tony's response: "Do you think I did it on purpose?"

That deflated *my* balloon. Of course I didn't think he intentionally dragged me up and down those ramps in three-inch heels. He had made a mistake, simple as that, and he was truly sorry. He hated that his forgetfulness had put me through all this stress and pain, and before an important meeting as well.

Here is a man who loves me more than the world, would do anything for me, and would never intentionally put me through any kind of agony. And I was accusing him of setting up a "find the car" wild-goose chase.

It is understandable that when someone you don't respect or like does something wrong, you are unlikely to see it as a mistake. For instance, when a politician you oppose gets caught doing something wrong, you know they meant to do it, and you use this information to legitimize your low opinion of this person. However, when *your* candidate gets called on bad behavior, you'll probably see it as an isolated incident or an oversight.

Your spouse should be treated at least as well as your favorite candidate. Most likely, he is probably more deserving of the benefit of the doubt than the politician.

The important point here is to see your partner's transgressions as mistakes—not deliberate, personal slights or attacks on you. If you remember and act from knowing that you are both really on the same side, you will see a very different response from them and a more satisfying outcome to the argument.

Rule #2: Stick to the Facts and the Issues

If you remember the old television series *Dragnet,* you remember that every crime victim or witness wanted to tell Sergeant

Joe Friday a long story about what happened. They'd usually
start out telling him what they knew, but before long they were
off on their great aunt Bessie and how it all related to "those
people down in Washington" and Joe Friday would have to drag
them back to reality with "Just the facts, ma'am."

You won't get anywhere in an argument until and unless you
stick to the facts and the issues at hand. Dragging in every past
incident or attacking every personality trait is only going to take
you farther away from a happy ending and closer to "irrecon-
cilable differences." As human beings, we can't handle every
incident and character defect at one time. There is just no way
we can respond to that much input. We can, however, respond to
and deal with a solitary incident.

Let's say I get angry at Tony for not giving me a phone message. This can quickly snowball to include how insensitive he is,
how he doesn't respect my work enough to write down messages,
that he is completely nonsupportive of me, jealous, unconscious,
and irresponsible. I then can bring up a slew of past incidents
that prove any or all of these points. And I can put the final nail
in his coffin by boasting how *I* always write down and give him
his messages.

I may score the most points toward winning this argument—
heck, I may even be right—but in the long run (and this relationship is for the long run, remember) I'm not likely to be
satisfied. This is called winning the fight but losing the game.
What do I really want to *get* out of this argument? Most likely,
it's not winning the argument but having Tony realize how much
this means to me and feeling so sorry that he'll never forget to
give me a message again.

If I go for winning the argument, Tony will most likely be
goaded into defending himself by taking a few shots of his own
at me. And he will be bitter and resentful toward me for
the attacks I have made on him. Fighting back, he may say,

"Well, your messages aren't important. All you do is gossip anyway!"

Even if I do win the argument, I probably won't get much satisfaction or relief because, overall, I will end up feeling bad about the hurtful and unfair things I said. So, in winning, I'm not getting the result I wanted in the first place, I'm just adding some new sensations of regret and resentment to my original feelings of anger and hurt.

When you find yourself looking for as much ammunition as you can to use against your spouse, take a breath and ask yourself, "What do I really want to accomplish here?" Then stick to the facts and the issues at hand. You can fully express your feelings, but *be specific*. What exactly are you angry about this time, this incident, and say why you feel so strongly—don't pull in the past or some unrelated side issues. The same rule applies when your spouse is angry with you. Ask what he or she wants as an outcome of the argument, and then stick to the specific facts and issues at hand.

Rule #3: Leave Others Out of It

This is probably the most damaging thing you can do in a fight. *Never* bring another person into an argument to take your side, *especially* when that person is not even present.

For some reason, this escalates arguments into the stratosphere more than any other thing I know. If a husband says, "Even Steve told me he thinks you're too hard on the kids," something snaps. Paranoia sets in: "Is everyone talking about me, does everyone think I'm an awful mother, am I so awful they can't tell me themselves?" Off you go, away from the argument at hand, feeling cut off at the knees by someone who is not even there to verify the story.

Not only is this taking unfair advantage, it can do serious damage to your relationship with the absent third party. (I don't have to bring your mother-in-law in as an example to make my point, do I?)

Tempting as it may be, it's unfair fighting, unsportsmanlike conduct, and, above all, it doesn't work. You and your partner need to be able to resolve your disputes on their own merit, not on the accumulated weight of other people's opinions and points of view.

Rule #4: Apologize

One of the simplest, most powerful tools in the area of relationships is an apology. It is also one of the most difficult to use.

This is not because we all believe the line from the movie *Love Story* that "Love means never having to say you're sorry." No, we don't like to apologize because we don't like to admit that we were wrong. It sounds silly but it's not. I've known people who were more willing to walk away from good marriages than they were to say, "I'm sorry."

Apologizing doesn't have to mean succumbing, caving in, or even admitting you're wrong. It could mean, "I made a mistake. I did (or said) something that caused you pain, and I am sorry for that." Certainly, if you have done something wrong (and who hasn't) you need to own up to it and apologize. This is not caving in, this is being an adult and having the honor and dignity to take responsibility for your actions. If you don't, you end up defending behavior you do not want to be associated with.

Let's say you didn't do anything you thought was wrong, so you don't feel the need to apologize. You signed your son up for a scuba diving class, and your wife is furious at you for spending the money. Even after hearing her tirades you still think it was the right thing to do, and you don't believe you should apologize for doing the right thing. What you can apologize for, however, is having done something that upset her.

This is not about pretending you're sorry and giving a fake and insincere apology. And it's not saying you're sorry that you did what you did. Instead, you're saying you're sorry she's upset or he got hurt. After all, you are sorry, aren't you?

This way it is easier to say you're sorry and mean it. An apology is not the end of the conversation, but it clears the air and provides an opening for you and your spouse to get back on the same side. Then you can begin to deal with whatever the real issue is (in this example, your differences on spending money) in a rational way.

Rule #5: Be Authentic

Saying "I'm sorry" is usually a great tool. However, some of those who know how effectively it can be used to defuse inflammatory situations are often in danger of abusing it. Tony is such a person.

Recently, Tony came home from a weekend with the guys and told me about a joke that got the most chuckles from this group of married men. "What are the most feared words a wife can say to a husband?" The answer is, "Honey, we need to talk." But for me it is what men say when they hear those five words that rings with the greatest truth: "What did I do?" Tony is more advanced than most husbands. At the slightest hint of irritation in my voice, he skips "What did I do?" and goes straight to "I'm sorry." Usually he gets away with this, but sometimes it just doesn't fly.

Once I was disturbed with how things were going between the two of us. I have very high standards for our relationship; I'm not interested in an ordinary, getting by kind of marriage. I told him how I felt and what I wanted. I even clarified for him: "I need more affection, and more expressions of love—out loud in words, and actions, like flowers, gifts, etc."

Tony, of course, quickly apologized and agreed with me. He could "see" that he hadn't been giving me these things, and that he "understood" what I was saying. "Yeah, yeah, yeah," he said. "I'm so sorry; it'll never happen again."

But did anything change? Did he hold hands with me at the movie? Did bouquets of flowers crowd my living room? Nothing. Rien. Nada.

From the chapter on communication, you know I think that you have no right to complain or be mad at your spouse for not giving you what you want if you don't let them know what that is. But I had been *very specific* with Tony.

He got home a couple of nights later to a note showing him to the guest bedroom. The final words to the note were "Don't you dare come to our room and say you're 'sorry.' You're not getting off that easily."

Tony came through the next day with flying colors. And from this experience I learned that before I accepted an apology from Tony I needed to make sure *he knew* what he was apologizing for, and that he was not using the apology to simply avoid or get rid of the unpleasantness.

Now I ask him what he thinks he's apologizing for and why he thinks I'm mad or hurt. I want to make sure the apology is authentic. Still, I have to hand it to Tony: Apologizing is a lot easier than going to battle over insignificant matters. And even though his apologies are sometimes automatic and not thoughtful, I admire him for always knowing what he really wants in life—a harmonious and supportive relationship.

Rule #6: Be Willing to Forgive

Your spouse apologizes. Now it is up to you to decide whether or not you are going to forgive him or her. Before you can forgive someone, you must understand that, ultimately, forgiveness is a gift. It is not something that has to be earned or deserved. It is not something to be bartered or traded in return for compliance to the promise of future corrected behavior. It is always yours to give or not to give. And like an apology, unless your forgiveness is authentic, don't give it!

Forgiveness means to "give as before," to be unconditionally willing to be with the other person in the same way you were before the transgression. This is easier said than done. Depending on the severity of the hurt and anger, it may take time before you're willing to clean the slate. Take your time! I'm not saying to wait until your spouse has been duly "punished" or proven him- or herself, but you need to wait until *you* are really ready to "forgive and forget."

So often I hear couples in my course bring up very old incidents when discussing their current problems. When I ask for details, they always tell me that the old incident was dealt with and forgiven long ago. I disagree. If the incident is still being talked about, forgiveness was never genuinely given. I know you *think* you forgave your partner for that past transgression, but if you find yourself bringing it up and using it against him or her in any way, you had better think again. You have not completely forgiven, and you are going to have to exercise considerable self-discipline to not use what happened against your partner.

When something is unforgiven between two people, however long ago it happened, the past hurt is carried forward into the present. Forgiveness does not erase what happened in the past, but it does restore you to the present free of the burden and pain of the past. Forgiveness is such a radical act that it is impossible to fake it, but it is quite possible to fool yourself. Because forgiveness is such a miraculous gift and because it can be so difficult to work through a painful issue and reach total forgiveness, I am including at the end of this chapter a four-step forgiveness process that you can use when you find yourself stuck and unable to forgive. It was designed by a friend who is a Catholic priest, and it really works.

One of the hardest tests of forgiveness is infidelity. Michael and Laurel had been married twenty-two years. Five years before they took my course, Michael had a one-night stand. He told Laurel shortly after the incident and she was devastated. They argued, cried, hashed it over for days and weeks. He begged her for forgiveness, and she finally gave it. Except in every argument thereafter she would bring it up again. If he forgot to pick up the dry cleaning as he promised, she screamed that this was further evidence that he was untrustworthy just like that time with "her." He never had a chance.

We went back to that original incident to see if she was really willing to forgive him—that is, to give herself to the relationship as before. In order to accomplish this, she would also have to *give up the right to ever use the past indiscretion against him again.* This is the key and most necessary component of forgiveness. When you truly forgive, what you are agreeing to is eliminating that particular incident or item from your arsenal in *all* future arguments.

I told Laurel I could understand if she considered infidelity unforgivable and couldn't forgive Michael. Forgiveness is a choice, not an obligation. It must be given freely. But if she didn't forgive him, her marriage was over. You can't have a relationship operate around such unresolved feelings and not have the affinity die. She knew I was telling the truth, because she'd been living it the past five years.

As it turned out, Laurel's love for Michael was so strong that when she looked at forgiveness as a gift, she was able to make that choice. Her difficulty before had been that she had been waiting for Michael to somehow make it up to her. And even though her love for him was as deep as it was, given the hurt from the betrayal, there was nothing *he* could ever do that would take away that pain. She saw it was up to her to let it go. And when she did, the pain and hurt of the incident also began to heal.

Laurel chose forgiveness, meaning she chose her marriage. They now have a loving relationship again, something that had been missing for more than five years.

Exercises in Creating What You Want

A. Write a list of everything for which you need to apologize to your spouse. List even stupid, insignificant things that "don't *really* warrant an apology"—like being the TV remote-control "hog" last night, or that you were ten minutes late for a lunch date last week. Go back as far as the beginning of your relationship. List as many things as you can and don't edit! If it comes to mind, write it down—anything you can think of, even stupid, silly things. More is better. Write, write, write!

   1.

   2.

   3.

   4.

   5.

and many more!

B. Make a list of those things for which you have not forgiven your spouse as well. Include those things you said you had forgiven but, in truth, you are still holding—and maybe even using—against him or her. As with the previous exercise, if a thought comes to mind, write it down.

1.

2.

3.

4.

5.

and many more!

C. Sit down with your partner and read to him or her from your two lists. You don't have to read *every* stupid thing you wrote—but why not? Ask your spouse to just sit and listen, not comment, discuss, agree, or disagree. You can do all that after you've finished reading your list.

D. If you need help or if you are not sure whether or not you have completely forgiven your partner for something, you can use this four-step process.

1. Are you willing to forgive? This is not a question you can answer by consulting your feelings or even your thoughts. Forgiveness is a choice and an exercise of your will. The answer to the question is either yes or no. When you are able to answer yes, you can go on to the second question.

2. Are you willing to forgive totally? Asking this question gives you the opportunity to fully remember what happened. As each memory is faced, you then have the opportunity to let it

go—or not let it go. Forgiveness takes place on your terms, not anyone else's. When you can answer yes, go on to the third question.

3. Are you willing to forgive absolutely? When someone or something is unforgiven, it is frozen in time and place. When you can answer yes to this question, what you have not forgiven begins to dissolve from its frozen state and there is even the possibility of what happened contributing to you. Then go on to question four.

4. Are you willing to forgive unconditionally? Forgiveness is a choice, not an obligation. Unconditional forgiveness is a gift, freely given, no strings attached. When you can answer this question yes, real healing of the hurt and pain begins. You won't forget what happened, and the facts will not change, but your memories and emotions will be healed and restored to wholeness. This is the miracle of forgiveness.

It would be easy to just read these exercises and then turn the page to the next chapter. The question is: Do you want an extraordinary relationship or are you willing just to sit back and see how it turns out? From the feedback I get from the couples who have taken my course, it was doing the homework that brought the incredible results they experienced. So stop, take the time, and write out these lists completely—then schedule a time to read them to your spouse—and then, and only then, turn to the next chapter.

Share the
Wealth

Money and sex are the two most highly charged issues in relationships. All of us have histories in these areas that run long and deep. Sex we'll talk about in the next chapter, but for now, the topic is money and how our attitudes and beliefs about money can undermine our relationships.

There is very little chance that you and your spouse are going to view money the same way. Money is like time: There are people who are always late (or short), and there are those who seem blessed with abundance and have more than enough. It is not that some people are born lucky, it's that people think differently about money. And while you can't make someone else relate to money the way you do, you can use a system that allows for your differing points of view. This chapter includes an exercise for developing such a system that will enable you to *never argue about money again.*

Tony and I are typical in our contrasting attitudes. With the same bank balance, I feel we have plenty of money, and Tony is certain we are not going to make it another month. Our arguments used to be frequent and predictable. I would argue that we had more than enough to take a vacation or do whatever I was advocating at the time. He just needed to be more optimistic, to have an attitude of abundance. He was too "negative" and his "scarcity mentality" was unhealthy for him and for our family's well-being. He needed to change.

Tony argued that whatever it was, we couldn't afford it, and it was irresponsible to spend beyond our means. The vacation was going to end up costing more (it always did), and besides, we still hadn't set aside money for the savings account, the IRA, or the kids' college tuition. And what if the payment we expected didn't come in next month? We wouldn't be able to cover our bills! As an accountant, he knew I was reckless with money, out of control, and possibly even dangerous.

These arguments were based on trying to get the other one to change his or her way of thinking about money—something that was never going to happen.

Stop Trying to Change Your Spouse

One day, Tony and I made a great discovery. We were out shopping, and Tony saw some shoes he liked. He said he really wanted them but couldn't afford them. I, of course, thought we could afford them and said he should buy them. But just at that instant, instead of going into my usual harangue about how we could afford the shoes, I realized that from Tony's point of view, we really *couldn't* afford them.

I said, "Tony, I know you can't afford the shoes but don't worry, I can. I'll buy them for you." It was an epiphany for both of us to see that neither person was wrong; we just had different points of view.

After that, I became more willing to forgo a vacation, not because I thought we couldn't afford it, but because I saw it would be too stressful on Tony to spend the money, so it wouldn't really be a vacation for him. Or Tony would agree to do something not because I had convinced him that we should spend the money, but because he thought it was important enough to me to be worth a little worrying on his part.

Stop the Arguments

Tony was raised in a family where money was scarce. I was fortunate to grow up in a home where money was more abundant. Over time we have developed an understanding and compassion for each other's beliefs. I respect Tony's determination to save money and plan for the future. He in turn credits me for the times we have made spending choices that were uncomfortable for him but have added value to our life together.

The arguments about money stop when you accept that you and your spouse feel differently, and you then let go of your belief that there is a right way or a wrong way to deal with finances. I know this is hard, because deep down inside you *know* you are right. You can even prove how right you are from your past experience and from all the books on finance. You may very well be right; however, you are not going to win the argument. In fact, you may lose what you think you are protecting— your marriage. At the very least, your precious time together, to love and enjoy each other, is being used up on these repetitive arguments that get you nowhere.

It's much easier and a lot more effective to try to understand your partner's point of view. (This is called compassion.) You don't have to agree with or give in to what they think, just understand it.

The Truth Is That You Want
Your Spouse to Have It All

What *must* exist in a loving relationship is an attitude of *wanting* your spouse to have, do, and be everything he or she wants. Just as you want the best for your children and for all their dreams to be fulfilled, you naturally want the same for the love of your life.

However obvious this may be, you still have to deal with three major obstacles that can get in your way: (1) your ideas about what is fair and not fair, (2) the confusion between trading and giving, and (3) fears your spouse will take advantage of you.

What's Fair?

How many times do parents respond to the complaint "But that's not fair!" with "Life isn't fair"? Yet we are still comparing the sizes of our piece of cake to that of the person sitting next to us—even when the person happens to be our spouse.

I went horseback riding one evening with a girlfriend. When we were out on the trail she asked me what Tony had said when I told him I was leaving him at home with the kids while I went riding. I told her Tony was happy for me and had genuinely said, "Have fun!" when I left. She was surprised. In her relationship, the unspoken rule is that if her husband is working, she is not supposed to be having fun. It wouldn't be fair.

People are often the same way about money. "If *you* are going to buy a boat, *I* get to buy a new car." "You bought those new CDs, so I'm getting a new coat." There is nothing inherently wrong with this except the point of view is one of "looking out for me" rather than giving and generosity. You're not looking at what's going to make your spouse happy, and you are not expressing love. You are watching what your spouse is spending so that you can be sure you get just as much for yourself.

My goal is for Tony and my children to have everything they want. (There are exceptions, of course—like a twenty-year-old blonde for Tony and the semiautomatic rifle my son keeps asking for.) Nothing gives me more genuine pleasure. When we only look out for ourselves, we miss the incredible feeling we get from expressing our love for our partner through giving.

The other thing I've observed over the years is that when I am more focused on giving than on getting, somehow the things I really want come to me.

When I first moved to Santa Fe, I was leasing a horse and taking riding lessons almost daily. I was in heaven! Then, after about a year in Santa Fe, we experienced a financial slump. I came home one day from riding and told Tony, given our situation, I didn't think it was appropriate to continue my riding. I especially didn't think it was worth the added pressure it put on Tony as he worries more about money. He was relieved and touched by my decision. He said, knowing how much I loved riding, he would never have asked me to give it up. (Tony always wants me to have what I love.) The next day a woman called me to ask if I could go riding with her. She needed someone to help exercise her horses. I've been riding her horses and others ever since. I didn't even go a week without my beloved riding!

Trading Is Not Giving

What most people consider "giving" could more accurately be called "trading"—and like "fairness," trading is looking at your relationship from the wrong direction. You are keeping score, putting a price on your generosity instead of freely giving. "I work and bring home the paycheck. In exchange, she takes care of the home and children."

How many times does it enter my mind to justify the time I spend having fun? "I got the kids ready for school, so I don't have to feel bad that Tony is picking them up. Therefore, I can go riding." There's nothing wrong with trading tasks and favors, but as a way of relating to each other it diminishes both partners and ultimately your relationship as well.

First, it implies that what you do, and particularly what you do for each other—in this case, getting the children ready for school or picking them up—is a chore or a burden. Tony and I feel so lucky to be parents that we love doing things like packing lunches and walking the children to their classrooms. Second, Tony wants me to have fun and enjoy myself; it makes him happy to contribute to my doing the things I love to do. If I look to his generosity as something he owes me or something I have to earn in trade, rather than as the gift it is, I rob myself of being nurtured by his love as much as I rob him of the pleasure of giving. In relationships run by the rules of commerce, everyone gets shortchanged.

You Might Get Screwed

The fear that your partner will take advantage of you, that you will give more than you get, will kill a relationship. Remember the old saying that it is better to give than to receive? Well, it's true. If you feel like you're not getting enough back, then you are not truly giving, you are trading.

I enjoy entertaining in my home. I love having friends over, hosting social events. And I always take an opportunity to celebrate a birthday (any excuse for birthday cake!). But I don't keep count of who has us over for dinner in return. I don't need reciprocation, because the experience of pleasure is already complete. In fact, it seems mildly insulting to be invited to someone's house just because they "owe" us a dinner.

We seem to instinctively guard against being conned, even in our most loving relationships. Time that could be better spent enjoying what we have is squandered on checking to see if we got the best or worst of the deal—as if we were haggling over trinkets in a tourist bazaar. To combat this fear, see where you can be outrageously generous. Do it in a way that you actually *try* to have someone take advantage of you. Hope it happens. You will find that when you are truly giving—not giving in order to get something back—you will simply become the richer and more nurtured.

Doing this goes against what I learned growing up. Nothing was more important to my father than making a deal and not getting taken. My father bargained over everything, including my allowance and my mother's grocery money. I'm not sure how I broke free of this pattern, maybe I was rebelling against my father, or perhaps it was my admiration for people who had a natural inclination to be generous. Whatever it was, I learned I wanted *that* quality and set about to discipline myself to acquire the skills I witnessed in others. It still requires conscious effort on my part to be this way. I often find myself wanting to be petty or cheap, but I'm always sorry when I succumb, just as I always feel better about myself when I don't.

There are many times in my marriage when I feel as if I'm not getting enough—enough affection, attention, respect, compliments, flowers, gifts—just not enough. At first when this happened, I would complain to Tony. Later, I learned I could make requests. Now when I feel deprived, I see it as a warning light telling me, "If I feel this way, Tony probably does, too." So I start to give to Tony whatever I feel I'm lacking, and guess what? In no time at all, it starts coming back my way. This works *every single time.*

In the same way, my policy on giving or spending money in relationships is to always err on the side of generosity. When in doubt, give more! Buy for them, give to them, spend on them whatever they want, as long as you can do it with no other reason or motivation than showering them with love. Contrary to what many people think, lavishing love on someone will not spoil them. It's only when gifts or money are given instead of love that more is expected and demanded, because you can never get enough of what you don't really want. Love is what is wanted and needed, and giving generously can be a beautiful and wonderful expression of that love.

Whose Money Is It Anyway?

Some couples tell me it works for them to keep their finances separate from each other. I am always skeptical when I hear this, but I am also for what works, and if that is what works, great. If I get to know these couples better, however, I usually discover their system of separate money reveals a lack of trust. And if I delve a little deeper, I often find resentment and very deep hurt.

Hilary and Justin had been married for twelve years and still kept their money separate. They split the mortgage and household expenses in half, as they did everything else. Justin was very generous on birthdays and anniversaries, but if they went out to dinner, it was quite natural for him to get the bill and say to Hilary, "Your share is twenty dollars."

During a workshop Hilary told me what she had never told her husband: Every time this happened it was "like Justin sticking a knife in my heart. It has nothing to do with the money. It is the feeling that he doesn't *want* to pay for me. Somehow it always makes me feel unloved and very, very separate."

After hearing this, I suggested that the way they were dealing with money was not nurturing their marriage. I told them they should combine their money. Justin hit the ceiling. He was terrified that Hilary would spend all of *his* money.

I pointed out that *not* combining their money was keeping them from getting closer, and it was creating an ever-widening crack in the foundation of their marriage. Instead of growing stronger with time, the relationship was slowly disintegrating. Ultimately, they agreed to my suggestion and set up a money management program like the one described at the end of this chapter.

Six months later, when I saw Hilary and Justin again, they both remarked at the profound change in their relationship from such a "simple little thing like sharing our money." Justin said, "I thought I had vowed to share my life with Hilary when we married. Well, I was full of it. Sharing my life means sharing it all. What surprised me when I did finally give in was that it wasn't the sacrifice I thought I'd be making. Instead, it's been freeing—I feel more myself. Before I felt I always had to watch every penny to make sure everything was equal, now I feel less suppressed. And I even feel richer—in fact, I am. After all, now we have two incomes! But the best thing is that we are more in love than we've ever been. Getting through this process was not easy, but the closeness and trust we now share was more than worth it."

Lighten Up a Little, It's Only Money

When my father died I inherited some money. Tony, who has a degree in accounting, was advising me on how to handle what was my "separate property." As he was outlining a plan, I interrupted him and said, "Honey, let me give you some advice. If you had inherited this money I would treat it as my own, so I suggest you do the same." He laughed and said, "You would, wouldn't you?" That was the beginning and end of our separate money.

Tony and I do not hold back from each other, and that includes every aspect about how we deal with money. What's his is mine and what's mine is mine. Whoops, sorry, I sometimes just can't help myself, but you get the point. Relationships structured around handling money as "mine" and "yours" may avoid some conflicts, but they introduce a structure of separateness. Since one of the biggest problems in marriages is the tendency to grow apart, anything that works against the flow of moving closer is detrimental. If you cannot find a way to operate as partners around money, you will be working against your goal of strengthening and deepening your relationship.

Your Money and *Your Life*

This "sharing" of money is much more significant when one person comes into the marriage with major wealth. In these cases, every attorney who works on an hourly basis will advise you that a prenuptial agreement is absolutely essential. Lawyers, of course, are not known for supporting relationships or for any great wisdom about them. I don't advocate ignoring legal advice, I just want you to be clear about your purpose in establishing a prenuptial agreement and the consequences. Fundamentally, I don't believe in prenuptial agreements, because they contradict the marriage vows. You are not being completely truthful if you say you are willing to love and cherish this person above all others, to give yourself completely to them, and then, out of the other side of your mouth, say, "but you are not getting your hands on my money."

Of course, it's appropriate to protect your estate for your children and other family members. But as I have already said, the more separation you create with your money the more separation will be created in the relationship. If you are going to set up a prenuptial agreement, you need to be very careful how you do it, so that in the guise of protecting yourself you don't destroy what you should be holding as most valuable.

If you do choose to have a prenuptial agreement, it is extremely important to still have money you share as a couple. Nothing is more demeaning than one member of a couple controlling the purse strings and, therefore, using this to control their spouse. This will never engender love, trust, and true partnership.

The point here is to stop withholding in your relationship, to stop protecting yourself, and to trust your partner. You cannot commit to sharing your life without also sharing your money. It may be difficult to trust and to let go, especially if you have a history of being burned, but to the degree you hold back and guard your money, you will restrict the possibilities of love in your marriage.

OK, It's "Our" Money,
Now Who's Responsible for It?

In every relationship, one person is more concerned with the management of funds than the other. Often this is because one person feels the need to dominate by having control over the money. But it's also a natural way of being in relationships— just as one person may take more responsibility for the children, or for handling household repairs, vacation planning, or dinner preparation. It's unnecessary to double-up, but that doesn't mean that the partner who is not in charge of the finances should be irresponsible or unhelpful.

In our case, Tony assumes the role of managing our finances. As a certified public accountant, he is a natural for the job and he enjoys it. I have learned, however, not to abdicate all the responsibility to him. It's not that I don't trust Tony to do a good job, it's just that as his partner, I cannot abandon him to a job that at times can be a lonely burden.

How we handle this is by sitting down together at the beginning of each month and reviewing what was spent, what checks are about to be mailed out, where we stand in terms of cash balances, and so on. Tony likes to do this with me because he feels my input is critical, especially in those times of near crisis when he doesn't want to make the "life and death" decisions by himself. Somehow, doing it together makes something unpleasant much more workable.

Whose Job Is It to Make the Money?

Every relationship is different. In some cases, the husband and wife both work and both have equal incomes. But more often one spouse, usually the husband, earns more. When this happens, it can bring up the "what's fair?" issue again.

Instead of keeping score on who brings how much to the table, you need to look as a couple at all the different factors that affect what is going to work best for your relationship and for your family. Tony and I have both worked at times and, at other times, we have each taken time to be primarily responsible for the children. Tony loves to be with the kids, but he is happier and healthier when he has a challenging and consuming job outside the home. I'm the opposite: I am happier when I am working but the majority of my time is in the home.

Then there are individuals who will always earn more or less than their spouse by virtue of their profession or career choices. And there are many couples where the husband decided to stay home because what he made in his job hardly paid for child care, or the woman went back to work because the family needed more than one income. The deciding factor needs to be not what is equal and fair but what will nurture and support you as individuals, as a couple, and as a family.

Fred and Linda were having trouble with this. Fred didn't mind that he earned a lot more than Linda, but he thought she should earn at least $1,000 a month. Linda worked as an independent contractor and her income varied considerably from month to month. Admittedly, she didn't work much and spent a lot of time during the discussion justifying why she didn't produce a consistent income. Fred didn't want to talk about the fact that they didn't need the extra money. "That's not the point," he said, "it's the principle that's important here!"

I had known this couple for a long time, and I knew this disagreement was going nowhere. Finally I told Fred, "Listen, you and I both know it would be ten times easier for you to earn an extra $1,000 a month than to count on Linda doing it. I know you love and adore her, and you know she's very capable of earn-ing a lot of money, but it probably isn't going to happen—certainly not on a consistent basis. So I recommend you give up and stop driving yourself and her crazy." He burst out laughing because he knew I was right. He realized that he was wasting a lot of effort on something that wasn't going to work anyway. It was all about proving a point and going after "justice" rather than nurturing the relationship.

A Game Plan

Remember, a loving relationship includes wanting your partner to have and do what he or she wants. Think about that again for a moment. Any other opinion or point of view is likely to be manipulative, jealous, or selfish. If money were no object, can you think of something your spouse wants that you wouldn't want them to have?

But how do you deal with the fact that however much you would like to give your partner the world, there are limited funds in your bank account? The following Money Management System came from a course called More Money developed by John Garner. It will not only help you with these concerns, but if you follow the steps and continue to use this system after the initial round, it will end your fights over money forever. This may seem impossible, but it's been tried and proven. Your new problem will be what to do with all the spare time you used to spend arguing about money.

A Money Management System That Really Works

Schedule several hours together when you won't be disturbed. The time required varies, but allow yourselves at least three solid hours. Make a commitment to each other to stick with it until it's complete and to abide by the end result. Don't say you will go along with this plan while in the back of your mind you know you are not going to do your part. The discussion may get intense, but trust me, if you stay with it, your fights about money will stop.

STEP 1. Write down everything you spend money on each month. Put these in general categories such as groceries, rent or house payment, taxes, auto, household expenses, entertainment, clothes, kids, travel, etc. Next to each category write down approximately how much you spend. If some of these items are only paid annually or semiannually, such as taxes or insurance or maybe a vacation, then pro-rate them on a monthly basis.

STEP 2. Calculate your monthly minimum by adding the figures in Step 1.

STEP 3. Each of you make your own list of the major items you would *like* to spend money on. Some examples are: a new house or renovations on your current home; buying a car, boat, motorcycle, or motor home; savings, investments, eliminating debt, retirement funds, college funds, insurance; vacations, educational experiences, luxurious hobbies or collections. From your lists, each of you pick the *five* things you want most.

STEP 4. Combine your lists and eliminate duplicates. Your combined list should not have more than ten items and I recommend you try to narrow it down to four or five Remember these are your highest priorities, not just a wish list.

STEP 5. We now are going to create bank accounts and name them. (Don't rush to the bank yet, we're still just at the organizing stage.)

The first account is called the *Operational Account;* this will be your clearinghouse. All income is deposited into this account.

The second account is called your *Household Account.* The regular monthly expenses listed in Step 1 will be paid from this account.

The third account is called *Annual Expenses.* This is for items such as insurance or taxes that are paid once or twice a year.

The fourth and fifth accounts are your *Personal Pleasure Accounts.* You each have your own. These are *not* for the list you made in Step 4 but for those things you personally want to spend money on without having to explain or justify. For me, it may be the occasional impulse to buy a new pair of shoes; for Tony, it may be the annual fee for the tennis club. My girlfriend calls this account her WAM account, which stands for Walking Around Money. This account permits you to be impulsive, extravagant, and autonomous. This is also the account from which you buy each other presents.

The remaining accounts are the ones for your Step 4 list and should be named by the items or categories you've agreed on.

STEP 6. At the beginning of each month, take the amount you estimated for your monthly expenses out of the Operational Account and put it into your Household Account. This should be a checking account and is the account you will use for your daily and monthly bills and expenses, including ATM withdrawals. Then take the monthly amount needed to meet annual or semiannual expenses out of the Operational Account and put it into a separate savings account so you have it when those bills come due.

STEP 7. The remaining money in your Operational Account (if there is any) will be divided among the other accounts by percentage. This is where the negotiations begin.

I'll use Tony and me to illustrate. Other than the Operational and Household Accounts, we have established five other accounts:

Tony's Personal Pleasure
Nita's Personal Pleasure
Investments/Savings
Travel/Vacations
Kids' Education

As a starting point, I suggested we divide excess money equally among the accounts, giving 20 percent to each account. If we had $100 above household and annual expenses that month, each account would get $20. Tony, however, did not think personal pleasure was as important as investments and savings, so he proposed the following:

Tony's PP: 10 percent
Nita's PP: 10 percent
Investments/Savings: 30 percent
Travel/Vacations: 20 percent
Kids' Education: 30 percent

I could see Tony's point, but no way was I going to give up any more of my Personal Pleasure Account. This was the account I would use for clothes, and I needed every penny I could get my hands on. This is where creativity and knowing and understanding each other and a sense of humor come into play. I said to Tony, "Why don't you give up 10 percent of your Personal Pleasure making the Investments and Education funds 25 percent each, that's almost 30 percent." His response was, "That's not fair! Why should I give up 10 percent and not you?" My response, which hit the nail on the head was, "Because, Tony, you get personal pleasure out of investments and savings, I don't."

So we settled on the following:

Tony's PP: 10 percent
Nita's PP: 20 percent
Investment/Savings: 25 percent
Travel/Vacations: 20 percent
Kids' Education: 25 percent

After we did this process, discussions and arguments about money ended. Of course, there have been many, many months when nothing went into any accounts except the Household Account and the savings account for annual expenses. This caused concern but not arguments. Our money started to handle itself automatically, almost like a computer.

Before we did this, Tony *always* worried that if he didn't keep me in check, I would not only spend every penny we had but put us into serious debt. I, on the other hand, used to feel I had to battle for everything I wanted and, like a rebellious prisoner would at times strike a blow for freedom by spending money anyway. With this system, Tony no longer has to be the "bad" guy and I no longer feel a need to rebel. The controls, limits, and freedoms are already established and don't have to be reinvented every time a purchase is made.

STEP 8. Once you have agreed upon the percentages, set up the accounts. In our case we had eight accounts.
1. Operating
2. Household
3. Annual Expenses (taxes, insurance, school tuition)
4. Tony's Personal Pleasure
5. Nita's Personal Pleasure
6. Investments/Savings
7. Kids' Education
8. Travel/Vacations

It is difficult for some people to come up with funds in excess of the Household Account. But use those times to gain more clarity on where you stand financially, to set goals, and to create a game plan for success.

Inevitably there will be transgressions or break-downs—for example, purchases made from the Household Account that really should have come from a Personal Pleasure Account. Meet each month to go over your finances and discuss the transgressions. Either make the correction by replenishing the Household Account from the Personal Pleasure Account, or use this as a time to practice being generous with your spouse. Remember to keep your relationship clean by being honest. In money matters, as in every area of your relationship, the important thing is always to tell the truth.

Setting up this system can be tedious and time consuming, but in the long run we spend a lot less time now managing our finances and arguing or being aggravated with each other. As I've said many times already, I consider my relationship extremely precious and dear. To me, fighting over money spent on golf clubs or a lunch in a fancy restaurant is a tragic waste of time.

Exercises in Creating What You Want

A. Do something unreasonably generous for your spouse at least three times this week. (I gave this assignment during a course and one of the husbands purchased flowers for every single room of the house. When the couple told the group at the next session, it was obvious to everyone that while the wife, as the recipient of the gift, was thrilled, she was not the one who got the most pleasure. You should have seen the excitement and joy on that man's face—he was the ultimate picture of the ecstasy of giving.)

B. Have a discussion regarding money. If you had $20 million, what would you do with it? (Each partner tells his or her own plan.)

C. Write two Hot 100 lists (one for you personally and one for the relationship). These are the things you want—things, not qualities. It may be a stretch to think of a hundred items, but go for it. Don't worry about whether you really want it or not; this isn't etched in stone. Lists can contain something as inexpensive as a new notebook for a journal to as grand as owning your own town. Have fun!

D. Write down your financial goals for your relationship over the next year.
   1. What you would like to earn for the year, and
   2. What you would like to spend it on.

E. Set up your Money Management System. This system works. Hundreds of couples are using it with amazing results. If you have recurring disagreements around money, you have to at least try this. You owe it to yourself and to your relationship.

Great Sex—
Ready or Not

According to a survey done by a "leading authority," most couples in America have sex ten times a month, or about two and a half times per week. They must have been polling newlyweds, because most couples I talk with are far off this mark.

Right or wrong, the statistic is interesting because the issue about sex (if there is one) is almost always about frequency. And it always seems to be tied to a complaint: "She doesn't want to as much as I do," or "He never wants to cuddle, he just wants sex," or "I know I *should* want sex as much as he does, but I just don't." Either there is not enough or too much. However it is, it should be different.

In almost all these instances, there is really no problem, only the perception of a problem. One person desires sex more often than the other person, and just as with money, neither of you is wrong. Woody Allen brilliantly demonstrated what happens in his film *Annie Hall*. On a split screen, the two lovers in session with their respective analysts are asked how often they make love. "Hardly ever," he says. "Maybe three times a week." "Constantly," she says, "I'd say three times a week."

Many couples keep score when it comes to sex, and it's easy to fall into an emotional pattern. The one who wants sex more frequently feels rejected when he's turned down repeatedly with excuses like these:

- "I don't feel turned on right now."
- "I'm too tired; I've had an awful day."
- "The kids are still awake."
- "Tomorrow, okay? I promise."
- "I have a headache."

The requestor feels he must beg for sex. (I'm using "he" in this example because this is usually the case, but not always.) This upsets and frustrates him so that when she finally does "give in," his anxiety level makes him impatient in his lovemaking. This provokes further accusations from his wife—"All you ever want is sex," "You never want to hold me and just be affectionate."

The partner who wants sex less frequently begins to feel hesitant to exhibit any affection at all for fear of exciting her partner when she herself is not in the mood. To be safe, she turns off *all* affection. Angry, defensive, and tense, she often feels trapped just going to bed, wondering if her wishes will be respected.

Another factor further complicates the issue, and that is the prevailing belief that you shouldn't have sex unless you want it. For example, for a woman to engage in lovemaking when she doesn't feel like it somehow wouldn't be right. We see this as a submissive act leading to negative feelings. These feelings range anywhere from thoughts of having been used or treated as subservient to thoughts as extreme as feeling "victimized" as a rape victim or prostitute.

The cycle is complete. We now have a couple who are frustrated, defensive, and afraid to make a move out of fear of what will happen. And neither partner is nurtured physically or emotionally.

Give It Up

In my relationship, Tony would like to have sex four times a day. (OK, so I'm exaggerating to make a point.) The thing is, I don't need sex as often as Tony apparently would like. One day I didn't feel like having sex when Tony did. When I said as much to him, his response was, "Why not, you know once you get started you'll enjoy it? You always do."

When he put it that way, I had to admit it was true. I'm the same way about many things. Skiing is one of my favorite sports, but on the mornings we leave I often hope it will be snowing so hard I'll have an excuse to stay home. Once I'm on the slopes, however, I'm in heaven. Knowing this about myself, I always push myself even when I don't feel like it at first.

I realized it doesn't have to be a big deal if he wants sex more often than I do.

But in the area of sex, like many women, I was holding on to my initial reluctance with a moral rectitude. And this righteousness wasn't doing anyone any good. To take care of Tony's needs and wants, which I was committed to doing, I needed to make sure he had enough sex to be content. I hadn't really thought much about the difference in our needs until Tony, in a gently teasing voice, made his point very clearly when he said, "Nita, I don't require much to keep me happy. Just a little bit of food, a little bit of affection, and a little bit of sex."

Just as with money, giving generously to your partner sexually is an expression of love. Instead of waiting to feel turned on, put your attention on taking care of the other person. It's very likely that you will get turned on in the process. For me and for many of the hundreds of people I've worked with, nothing is more sensual than giving to your partner in such a way that they become aroused and passionately excited about being with you.

Unsaid Sex

The one-hour talks you've been having every day are important as groundwork (or foreplay) for lovemaking. In fact, one of these sessions is a good time to communicate about sex itself. It may take a while, even a few weeks, before you're ready to broach the subject, especially the things you've been keeping from each other. But if your intent is to have a completely intimate relationship, you need to bring even those into the conversation.

It is very powerful and, yes, also very frightening, but you need to give each other permission to fully express and communicate the truth with the understanding that neither of you will be penalized. The "truth" includes what you feel, what you've thought, what you're afraid of, what you like and don't like, and what you've done. But if you are not fully open with each other, a clear pathway of communication won't exist. This doesn't mean that you have to blurt out every single thought you've ever had, just those things you've been intentionally holding back. Usually, we think we can be selective and withhold some things from our partner and express other feelings instead. But with emotions, when the gate is shut, it's shut. The dam builds up and then *nothing* comes out. When we hold back negative feelings, or any feelings, the positive ones also get locked out. (You may want to review "The Things You Don't Say" in Chapter 5.)

George, for example, decided not to tell his wife, Sally, that he had held hands with an old girlfriend at a recent company picnic. "It's not that big a deal," he rationalized, "besides, nothing happened. I'll just be protecting Sally's feelings if I don't tell her."

It's true, it wasn't a big deal. But our communication mechanism works in such a way that when George focuses his attention on not telling his wife this one minor item, it blocked his ability to express himself in other ways as well. He might be saying out loud to Sally, "I love you," but the little voice in the back of his head will at the same time be saying, "Should I tell her? Why can't I tell her? If I really loved her would I have done that? Maybe I should tell her. Nah!" That little voice becomes pervasive and clearly gets in the way of George's relationship with Sally.

Open up the gate and let the negative sentiments out. What will also be freed up are the positive expressions of love that have been dammed up and doing battle with the other emotions. Once everything is out, you will find relief and an ability to fully express those wonderful, tender feelings again.

I've had people say, "Well, I can't tell him this one. He'll never forgive me," or "This will ruin our relationship, and he'll leave me." Take heart, it hasn't happened yet with any of the couples in my courses who do come around and communicate *everything* to each other. They have incredible breakthroughs in their relationships—all from just being willing to tell the truth.

And you need to confess everything—even something as apparently threatening as affairs. Otherwise, every time you see your spouse, you are also facing a lie within yourself that will keep you from ever being totally present with him or her again.

Not only are you living with the lie, but you're also living with the guilt associated with it. You've gotten this far in the book, now it's time to really come clean.

There is no easy way to deal with something as serious as an affair, but if you confess it and get it out in the open, at least the two of you can deal with it together. On the other hand, if you keep it pent up inside of you, neither one of you can come to a resolution. And if you think time will make it disappear, you're wrong. It won't work.

Remember, suspicions are always worse than reality. If you don't know what's going on, it will drive you crazy. But if you know, you can deal with it. It's easier to deal with something real than with something imaginary.

In the film *Fatal Attraction,* the leading man and his family are terrorized by a woman with whom he had a brief affair. Most of the terror, however, would never have happened if he had confessed his transgression to his wife in the beginning. *Together* they would have been able to disarm the obsessed "other woman's" attacks. (Of course, that would have made for a lousy movie.)

You've Just Got to Start Flapping Your Lips

Once people in my courses start talking, they find it much easier than they imagined it would be. They quickly come to realize that *not* talking was the real problem. In fact, they are always shocked at how simple it is to correct problems they thought they would never be able to discuss openly.

After a year and a half of marriage, Larry suddenly wasn't interested in sex. His wife, Christine, was devastated. Did he no longer consider her attractive? Was he seeing someone else? Finally, as part of the course homework, she asked him why he didn't want sex as much. It was hard for him to get it out, but, eventually, he told her that, because he had gained weight, he didn't feel attractive and didn't want to risk her rejection!

This was much easier for Christine to deal with than her fears. Sure, she was concerned about his weight, she told him, but it certainly had no effect on her sexual interest in him. "Let me at you in bed," she said, "and I'll prove it to you."

Another woman in the same course, Beth, had never liked the way her husband, John, touched her—and they had been married for more than six years! How could she possibly tell him after all this time? John surprised her with a relieved laugh when she confessed. He couldn't believe she had waited so long to tell him. He was very understanding, open, and interested in how she did want him to touch her.

Even Jenny, who was petrified to tell her husband she'd had a brief affair three years before, was encouraged to bring up this horrible secret she had been harboring. I told her husband, Jack, that Jenny had something important to tell him, and he must agree to make it safe for her to do so. He agreed, but Jenny was still so nervous about his reaction she took him out in the hall away from everyone else. She was amazed at his calmness after she told him. Like John, he was relieved to understand the source of his wife's anxieties and sorry she hadn't been able to tell him sooner.

Some of us are very uncomfortable talking about sex. In order to do the exercise at the end of this chapter, one couple had to sit with their backs to each other. If you don't talk about them, the problems you are hiding will not go away. If you're keeping things back, you don't know what you *can* say anymore, so you don't say anything. And we all know by now that a relationship without communication ceases to be a relationship.

When you were first married, you felt like you could tell your spouse anything. That's what you loved. It's when you stop talking that the marriage doesn't seem fresh and new anymore. It's important that you handle the big issues that stop you from communicating, because this is the person you have chosen to spend the rest of your life with. I know it sounds risky to tell "all," but it's either that or settle for a mediocre sex life and a mediocre relationship.

The talks you have can actually be fun once you get over the initial fear. But if you feel you can't handle this alone, then you should seek counseling. There are a lot of qualified people who can help you reestablish communication and work through sexual problems. And visiting a counselor doesn't mean there is something wrong with you. In the past, our culture put a stigma on the need for counseling, but you shouldn't put up with serious problems when there are so many trained people who can give you professional assistance.

Flex Appeal

Sex is a critical and natural form of communication. One of the things that happens when people in my course begin having their one-hour talks is that the frequency of their lovemaking increases dramatically. When you really communicate with your partner, you naturally want to be closer physically.

National average or not, my own research has shown that having sex two and a half times a week *is* very healthy for a relationship. You don't have to schedule it, although some people do and that works fine for them. Just make sure you and your spouse organize your lives to allow you to get together intimately at least twice a week. It's impossible to make love this often and not have good communication.

It's not only important for a good marriage that you have sex frequently, but that you enjoy it, and that you communicate your needs to your partner. You must let him or her know what you like and what you don't like. There is no other way around it. You've got to talk to each other.

I want to say it again for emphasis: Having sex often is very healthy for a relationship. Once a month is not often enough, although some people think it is. For a relationship to be really strong and in great shape, you should keep up with the national average of two and a half times a week. Tony and I always joke about "what's the half?" Have fun trying to figure that one out.

A few years ago, Tony and I had just bought a home that required remodeling. We took on a large mortgage and all the tension and pressure that went with it. We weren't sure we could afford it, so we did what all red-blooded Americans do: We bought it anyway and then worried about it constantly. Everything went over cost. Tony would lie awake at night and fret over the financial stress. We became irritable and short with each other. I saw what was happening one sleepless night and realized that when we were really getting along and feeling good about each other, we could handle anything. The horrible part about this situation was not the circumstance, but that we were at odds with each other.

I told Tony that we had to get *ourselves* back in shape if we were to work our way through the problem. My plan was simple: have sex every night for a week. Tony was shocked that I would come up with this plan, but he was a pushover and agreed to give it a try. As it turned out, we didn't just go through the motions every night. We made a game of it. Tony wrote love letters and brought home flowers, and I had candles lit in the bedroom ahead of time. It was a hot and passionate week—and boy did we forget about the house! Of course, the mortgage didn't miraculously get paid off by a rich uncle, but Tony and I became love partners again! And within that context we were able to work together on resolving our financial problems.

The funny thing is, now that Tony knows my solution for relieving excess stress, he can't wait for the next crisis to hit!

Continuing Education

I recently had a revelation about how stunted we are as a society in the area of sex. In every other active aspect of our lives, whether it is work or pleasure, we do things to further our knowledge and expertise. In a profession, it might be classes to keep up credentials. In a sport or hobby, we all know to find an instructor to sharpen skills. If you are into skiing, cooking, dancing, or computers, you will at least occasionally take the time to do a clinic or class or read a few books about your area of interest. Improving our skills allows us to derive greater pleasure and success from our activities.

With sex, however, most of us receive little or no training in the first place, and our prudishness or embarrassment keeps us from pursuing further knowledge. By limiting ourselves, we become bound and stifled in an area that is potentially very rich as well as extremely fulfilling and nurturing. Ask yourself: Are you satisfied with your performance? Can you imagine contributing more to your spouse sexually? Are you receiving in a way that leaves you and your partner totally fulfilled? Can you see how your relationship could improve sexually? There is a world of growth, development, healing, and intimacy available to you for the asking.

And don't kid yourself. You need training. We all do. Admittedly, you may have to overcome some strong feelings of discomfort, but what's possible far exceeds whatever fears you might have. There is no greater arena for building intimacy and healing than through conscious lovemaking. I recommend everything; reading books, researching some instructive videos, working with a therapist, or taking courses. Relax and open yourself up, get over any inhibitions and resistance you have solely for the purpose of bringing more love, closeness, and affection into your relationship. And, most important, have fun!

Exercises in Creating What You Want

A. Regarding sex with each other:
   1. List any questions that you want to ask your spouse that you have been afraid to ask.
   2. List any sexual activities you've had that you haven't communicated.
   3. List anything you'd like to do with your spouse that you haven't done or haven't done lately.
   4. List anything you've wanted to say but haven't.
   5. List any requests you have, especially what you would like your partner to do differently.
   6. List anything you've thought of or fantasized about that you haven't told your spouse.

B. Now, sit down and communicate your answers to the above questions to your partner and encourage him or her to do the same assignment. You may think, "I could never let him know these things," or "He would never forgive me." You may be hesitant to share the answers. But remember, the extent you hold back in sharing is the extent to which the quality of love and passion in your marriage will be held back as well.

Before you trade answers, though, it's important that you make it safe for each other to communicate. So say to your partner, "Listen, you can say anything and I'm not going to use it against you, hold it against you, or punish you for it."

C. Set aside a night where you share sexual fantasies with each other. You don't have to act them out. Just talk about things you'd like to do. This is a good time to buy magazines like *Penthouse* and *Forum* and let your imagination run wild.

Fantasies are not always acted out, but a lot of them are. One couple who took the "Connecting" seminar, Edward and Susan, had always wanted to go to a motel that had mirrors on the ceiling, a vibrating bed, and X-rated movies on the television. They had a phenomenal evening, laughing and sharing the reality of their fantasy. Another man, Andrew, had always secretly wanted his wife, Anne, to wear sexy Frederick's of Hollywood teddies with garters. Anne was so excited to go shopping and pick up the lingerie! She'd never known this was his fantasy. Often *places* to have sex are the focal point. One couple had always wanted to have sex in the kitchen and did just that! The object of the assignment is to have *fun* and return a sense of the unpredictable to your relationship.

Get
Your Family Values
Straight

When I met Tony, I was quite certain I did not want to have children. I had been a teacher, and I loved kids, but I liked leaving them behind at the end of the school day. My credo was, "Children are great, I just don't want any in my house."

Somehow, after being with Tony for a couple of years, wanting children became a natural expression of our love for each other. This sounds corny, but it's what happened. I had not grown up knowing I wanted to someday be a mother, so I was taken aback that suddenly I was overwhelmed with the desire to have a baby.

After months of failing to conceive, I tried talking myself out of wanting a child. "We have such a great life without children. We go out every night, we travel all over the world. We'd have to give up so much of our lifestyle. I'm sure we can have a fulfilling life without children." I had some good arguments, but they didn't change my mind. I had caught the "baby bug" in a bad way, and the more we failed to conceive the more all-consuming my desire to be a mother.

Like many men, Tony was neutral about having kids. He thought he would probably enjoy being a father, but he seemed to go along with the process mostly because it meant so much to me. And what a process he subjected himself to! Everyone talks about the fun of trying to get pregnant; well, it was great until we started seeing a fertility specialist. Then it became a parade of poking, testing, and "simple" surgical procedures timed around my menstrual cycle, with Tony required to spend afternoons alone in the hospital "red room" with a stack of *Penthouse* magazines, a test tube, and the job of delivering on demand.

This two-year journey ended with the arrival of two magnificent children through adoption and more joy than I can even begin to express. Tony, who was "neutral" about having kids, got hooked on fatherhood the second our son Jordan popped out (we were at his birth). While it took me a couple of hours to bond, for Tony it was immediate. Witnessing the transformation of my husband into a father was as miraculous as the birth. Even today, twelve plus years later, Tony is more passionate about his children than anything else in his life.

Having It All

Tony is so delighted with being a father, I have to remind myself that he was not the motivating force behind having children. He only agreed to please me. He is living testimony to one of the themes I keep going back to, the "golden rule" of relationships: wanting your spouse to have everything he or she wants.

This does not involve any sacrifice or compromise on your part. Rather, it is the key to your happiness and to the health and well-being of your marriage. If the only thing you do for your relationship is live by this golden rule, not only will your marriage work, but your entire life will flourish as well.

It should be sufficient reason to do something just because your partner wants it. Instead, however, we usually try to convince, cajole, or even manipulate or trick our spouses to get them to do something we want. If you want your mother to spend the weekend, you don't say to your wife you know she hates your mother and you understand it's a burden having her in the house, but please do it because it is important to you. No, you start by defending your mother, saying she is not as bad as your wife thinks. You try sweet-talking her into the idea and convincing her that it will be to her benefit because your mother will help with the cooking and household chores. You might top off your case with a little guilt, saying how important it is for the children to be with their grandmother.

We forget we can and should circumvent the "manipulation" with: "Please, do this for me." This can and should be reason enough to do whatever your spouse is asking.

"What does all this have to do with children?" you ask. "You can't possibly mean I should agree to having a child just because my wife wants one? We're not talking about putting up with an irritating houseguest for a weekend, we're talking about a very, very long-term houseguest. A houseguest who will be a total, emotional, and financial burden. Why not just ask for my blood? Besides, she agreed when we got married that we wouldn't have kids. Why am I now the bad guy?"

These are strong and logical arguments. You would undoubtedly win your case in a court of law. You will not, however, win in your marriage. If your spouse wants a child, and it has become something he or she feels very strongly about, then you must accommodate. At the very least, you need to "grudgingly" agree to go along with it. "I'll do the bare minimum but it's your baby." This would be the lowest of roads to take, and I certainly don't recommend it. Not only would you be robbing your spouse and child of the gift of your love, you would be reducing the potential joy in your life as well. The best for all concerned would be to really get behind the idea.

Should I Also Jump Off a Cliff?

If you apply my golden rule to everything in life, you'd be in real trouble. As a mother might say to an infatuated daughter, "If he asked you to jump off a cliff for him, would you do it? Where do you draw the line?"

Of course there is a line, and where to draw it is not the subject of this book. Right now we are only talking about children, and the point is, if one of you has a passionate desire for offspring, then that is reason enough for the two of you to proceed.

I'm thoroughly against the idea of bringing unwanted children into the world. I also do not believe that all married couples *should* have children. But I know from my own experience and from the experiences of the many couples I have worked with, if just one person in a relationship has a real desire for a child, then *his or her* life will not be full and complete unless that dream is realized.

I will never forget a television interview I saw where a highly accomplished woman surgeon who had chosen not to have children because of her demanding career was asked, "Do you ever think you made a mistake by not having children?" Without hesitation, she replied, "Every minute of every hour, every hour of every day."

Her response went straight to my heart and I realized how

important it is to support a spouse's wishes about having a child. How painful it must be to discover you have married someone not committed to your happiness. It seems incongruous to me to be in love with someone and deny them something so elemental.

So, my advice is very clear. If your spouse is yearning to have children, regardless of what you thought would happen when you got married, you must concede. Find a way to make it work. Stop focusing on yourself, and do what it takes to make your partner happy.

Before you jump up and force your husband to read this chapter (it is usually the wife who wants a baby), let's take this one step further. Suppose your husband reads this book and knows he must demonstrate his commitment to your happiness and so agrees to "go along." The next thing I have heard many times is the wife complaining that he "doesn't want it as much" as she does, and "if that's the way he's going to be, then I don't want a baby after all!"

Please give me a break. You can't have it both ways. Just as your husband can't make you suddenly switch your feelings from wanting to not wanting a baby, you can't make him want what you want or want it as much as you do. You have got to give him some room.

I've found few men initially enthusiastic about being married and having children. You don't see publications called *Groom* or *Fathering*. I don't like to generalize, but you know it's true. Marriage and babies are not men's sports. Still, time and time again you find that, once the baby arrives, it's the men who melt as soon as they have the baby in their arms.

And Baby Makes Three

As soon as couples have children, there is a tendency to put their relationship with each other on hold. Babies grab every ounce of attention you have. First, there is the shock of this new being, created by you! It is undoubtedly the most wondrous experience in life. You don't want to miss a second of being with this child. And the love . . . I had no idea I could ever love anyone so much. It is simply overwhelming, magnificent, and delirious. Then, of course, a baby is totally dependent on and demanding of your time and attention. To be needed by a child fills a need in ourselves, our need to give love and nurture unconditionally. We become nurtured in the process because the needs for a baby can be easily understood, and we can succeed in fulfilling those needs.

During this time, a spouse can sometimes seem superfluous or even unnecessary—or, worse, their needs can become an added, unwanted burden. Most of the time, both spouses are so tuned into the child that they don't notice that the flow of love between them has ceased or diminished. And if this continues for too long, one day they look at each other and realize that, though they've spent time together, their relationship has disappeared.

Guilt and resentment can creep into the marriage, making things more difficult. One spouse might feel slighted or jealous of the attention the other spouse is giving to the child. The wife might feel "guilty" about not giving her husband enough attention, but at the same time, she doesn't feel she has the time or energy. And the husband can grow resentful that the child is pulling his wife away from him. Who will he hold this against, his wife or the child?

These situations can be turned around almost instantly. If

you have neglected your one-hour talks, now is the time to get back into it. It is CPR for your marriage, and it *must* be done the minute you notice something is missing. I know it is now much, much harder with a baby, especially one who doesn't sleep at night, to set aside one hour for conversation with your spouse every day. You'll want to put it off—until the baby is sleeping through the night, or until you can get away together, or until you feel human again. Your tiredness will cause you to think up every possible excuse. But you can't wait until "the kids are in college" before you start communicating again.

If you look at the divorce statistics, marriages aren't waiting until we have time to care for them. And when you let your relationship drift, you risk losing the adult love and support you need for the long, difficult process of being a parent. Finally, you need to "do it for the kids." More than anything else you have to offer them, your children need you to have a strong loving partnership. Their health and well-being depends on it.

The Kids Need You

More children are being raised by single parents in the United States than in any other culture in the world. I haven't read any study saying this is beneficial to children, although there are many studies and articles on how detrimental divorce and single parenting are to children. The overall extent of damage from this phenomenon is immeasurable, but it is clear to me that having a strong and loving relationship is not just for us adults. The kids need us desperately!

Given the importance of raising children in the best possible environment, which is to say a "whole family," perhaps we should return to the old-world way of staying together no matter what. But this, too, has raised a great deal of criticism because of the danger to children when raised in adversarial households. And, obviously, a reversal of cultural trends is not practical.

I think the answer is to *have the marriage work* for the sake of the children, if nothing else. By this I mean that the married couple should take responsibility for the health of their marriage in the same way and with the same level of commitment with which they naturally assume responsibility for the health and well-being of their children. When a child is ill, every caring parent will take whatever action is necessary—a trip to the doctor, bed rest for a day, a change in diet. Similarly, if something is unhealthy in the marriage, you need to respond with an equal sense of urgency and responsibility. If it's "broke," then fix it, instead of discarding your spouse for a new and improved model.

Here is a short list of what a strong, loving relationship gives your children:

1. Stability
2. Security
3. A great role model for relationships to take into their own lives. (Wouldn't it be great if they really believed without doubt or reluctance that marriages *are* loving, supportive, and respectful?)
4. The idea and example that problems in relationships can be mended.
5. The experience that relationships are not disposable, which makes *them* feel as if *they* are not disposable either.

You Don't Have to Choose

The good news is you don't have to choose between your spouse and your children. You need to care for both, and attention to each can benefit the other.

My husband once asked me what it takes to be a great husband. I started listing all the qualities I could think of and then realized they were all the things I love about Tony. (Much of what I came up with is in this book in one form or another.) I also remember telling him that being a fabulous father (which he is) is one of the major reasons I think he is such a "great husband."

It is more than simple admiration. I think it is very sexy to see Tony being a concerned, playful, and loving father to our children. Maybe I'm unusual, but when I see our daughter crawl onto his lap as though she owns it and she belongs there, or when I watch "the guys" pack for a fishing trip and turn down my help because "they can handle it," I find myself kvelling (a Yiddish expression of being overcome with love) for Tony.

I also see a pride emerge in my children when I say my relationship with Tony is wonderful. They might turn away and say "Yuk!" when they see us embrace, but when we are in tune with each other I can see the confidence and calm in the faces of my children. They'll often ask why they're not coming with us when we go out or on vacations without them. I used to worry they'd feel I didn't want to be with them, but they always understand. And I believe they are even comforted by how much their parents love each other.

My daughter loves the times Tony brings me flowers or makes some other romantic gesture. Right now in her development she thinks Mom is the greatest, so she is affirmed when she sees how much her father loves her mom. And when I travel, she is the

one who reminds Tony they must go together and buy flowers
for my return.

Recently, at a parent meeting for my son's sixth-grade class,
Erin, mother of one of the girls, broke down in tears. She said
she had something to say to the parents of the boys in the class.
The makeup of the class was twelve boys and two girls, and since
my kids go to a small school where the same group has been
together since first grade, this same girl/boy ratio has existed
from the beginning. When we saw Erin's tears, we all thought,
"Oh, no. Have they been picking on the girls?" What we heard
instead shocked us. Erin thanked the parents for the way the
boys treated her daughter. She went on to say that her daughter's self-esteem had been greatly enhanced by the respect and
concern with which the boys treated her. She knew, as did we,
that these boys behave this way as a reflection of the way we, as
individual parents, relate to each other in our marriages.

Jordan looks up to me and treats me in a way I thought only
happened in story books and movies. The type of respect and
love my son shows me certainly wasn't present in the home
where I grew up. My brothers were mirror images of my father
and made fun of or put down my mother every chance they had.
They grew up in this mold and now continue their "learned"
behavior toward their own wives. Just as my brothers behave
the way they were brought up, so does my son, who has the benefit of having parents who admire and adore each other.

I am convinced the well-being of children is largely a function
of their environment, and it is parents who determine that envi-
roment. When parents openly display love, respect, and admiration for each other, their children are the primary beneficiaries.
So, if your children are important to you, and I'm sure they are,
you need to do whatever is necessary to maintain the quality of
your marriage.

Take Time for the Two of You

One thing that needs to happen to keep your relationship intact is for the two of you to take time to be together away from the children.

I know this is not practical for many. Baby-sitting services may be difficult or expensive to obtain, and scheduling may be complicated. But time alone is not a luxury, it is a basic requirement for the health and longevity of your marriage. Support the marriage of a friend or neighbor by trading off and taking care of each other's children, make lunchtime dates or meet while the children are in Sunday school, but make "your time together" a priority. Don't fool yourself. More than half the marriages today end in divorce. You are going to have to make an effort to beat those odds.

When They Are Not Your Children

This is a real source of problems in many relationships. It sometimes takes time for your relationship with his or her kids to develop, and it may never be wonderful. Workable may be the best you will get.

You are not required to like your stepchildren, and they don't have to like you for you and your spouse to have a healthy relationship. It is important, however, to make it clear to the children (and to yourself) that you aren't trying to replace their natural parent. That doesn't mean you can't establish limits or ground rules for how the children are to behave when they're with you. But don't try to parent another person's child and don't offer unsolicited advice about parenting, even if you think you know best. In other words, stay out.

If you both have kids, it can definitely get complicated. There are professional counselors who specialize in dealing with the problems that frequently occur in "blended" families. If you're experiencing difficulties, don't wait to seek out this kind of help. By getting support earlier rather than later, you can learn skills that will help you get past the challenges of the situation and prevent a lot of pain.

And Even When They Are

I am not going to give advice on child-rearing. I do know that if you apply the advice from the other chapters of the book to the dynamic of raising children, it will work equally well. If you are still having problems in working together as parents, however, it is crucial to seek professional support. This is a primary area of your relationship and cannot be swept under the carpet. Even if you get along in every other area of your marriage, if there are unresolved issues around child raising, the difficulties will seep into the "good" areas and destroy the relationship.

The expansion from couple to "family" creates a whole new dynamic in marriage. It makes the connection of the partners even more profound and purposeful. Accordingly, with more people, more personalities, and more personal agendas, even those of a two-year-old, everything becomes more complex with more opportunity for problems. But it is these same complexities that give rise to the possibility of richness that is available only through the experience of family—one many of us have been looking for our entire lives.

Exercises in Creating What You Want

This is a good time to catch up on unfinished exercises from previous chapters. Or it might be the night to create your own
answer to the question of what makes up the .5 in the statistical
average 2.5 times a week married couples have sex.

Don't Go It
Alone

Our parents and grandparents did not have to rely solely on each other to figure out how to have their marriages work. It was not uncommon for them to live with their parents, and uncles and aunts were usually just a few steps away in the same neighborhood. So when couples ran into snags in their marriage, there was always a relative nearby only too happy to pass on some wisdom.

In comparison to the "good old days," contemporary couples live in a vacuum. Although we may have close friendships with many people, the experience of extended family and community is harder to find. Even if you are an exception to this condition, advice from older members of the family or community often doesn't seem relevant. There have been too many changes in our culture and in the dynamics of our relationships for our parents to serve as contemporary role models.

The whole institution of marriage is in a state of evolution and change. The roles of husband and wife lack the definition they had only two generations ago, and the benefits we hope to find from relationships are completely upside down compared to earlier times. And unlike our parents and grandparents, we don't feel the *need* to marry in order to survive and be socially accepted.

Where it once might have been valid for a mother to tell her daughter to look the other way when her husband strayed, most women would reject such counsel today.

We're on Our Own

As a result of these changes, couples have no replacement for the old family support system and are left on their own, without mentors or trusted guides. This isolation is reinforced by the general belief that it is a sign of weakness to get help or it is wrong "to air your dirty laundry in public."

We are left with millions of stoic couples residing in individual homes, practicing self-reliance and trying to reinvent the wheel called a "successful, modern marriage." Judging from the divorce statistics, we're not doing too well. Almost everyone has had the shocking experience of one day talking with someone we consider a close friend and the next day hearing he or she is getting a divorce, and we never had a clue they had been having problems.

This happened to Tony with his close friend and jogging part-ner, David. Tony and David had been running together five mornings a week for four years. Out of nowhere, during one of their morning runs, David announced he was getting divorced. Tony had known David and his wife for fifteen years, had been with them as recently as the weekend before, had even run with

David the day before, and he had no idea that they were even considering separating!

Once he got over the initial shock, Tony said his reaction was: "I was delivered a fait accompli and there was nothing I could do to help. *I* felt defeated; I hadn't even had a chance to support him. What kind of friend was I that he couldn't talk to me, that he didn't feel he could come to me for help?"

Unfortunately, Tony's experience is not uncommon.

There Is Support Out There

Years ago, in my work as a management consultant, I discovered it was usually only the most successful businesspeople who hired consultants. There was a direct relationship between a person's degree of success and his or her willingness to seek consultants and outside support. Today, the "I can do it on my own" attitude is virtually nonexistent among powerful business executives.

The same is true in sports. Of course, team sports are always coached, but also at every big individual event from tennis to horse jumping, you find the athletes working with personal coaches or trainers. Many amateurs train on their own, but you'll never see the world-class ones without a coach.

Given my commitment to having a lasting and extraordinary marriage, it seemed to me the principle and value of having a coach would apply to relationships as well. So I decided not to go this one alone. This may have been the wisest decision I ever made. If there were medals given for superb performance in marriage, I think Tony and I would have accumulated several gold medals. And like any athlete who has just won, I have God and my coaches to thank.

Besides attending several of the classes and workshops I mention in the last chapter of this book, I've asked many individuals to support our marriage. Our closest friends, Terry and Alan Axelrod, were doing this for us even before we got married. They are ten years ahead of us in the marriage business, so almost everything we go through they've already been through. It's not even so much that Terry and Alan have the answers (although they usually do), it's having the counsel and perspective of someone you trust who is equally committed to the success of your relationship.

One of my most precious memories in our marriage is of the time my father passed away. I had gone to visit him in Phoenix because he was not well, but I had no idea how serious his condition was. Soon after I arrived at the hospital, it became apparent he would die within hours. I called Tony in Seattle and asked him to please get on a plane as quickly as possible. Tony told me later that the first thing he did after getting off the phone with me was call Terry. He told her, "I don't just want to go to Phoenix to hold Nita's hand, I want to be completely there for her. Tell me what to do."

Terry got the job done. She told Tony to make me talk to my father, even though he was in a coma, to make sure I said everything I needed to say to him before he died. Tony did this in an amazing way. Every time I stopped talking he would urge me to say more: "Tell him what you loved about him as a father, tell him what it was like for you as a child, tell him what you'll miss about him." Tony made sure nothing was left unsaid.

Terry also told Tony to take all the details away from me. He dealt with the doctors, the transporting of the body, our travel arrangements, and all the details of the funeral and closing up my father's house in Phoenix. Terry's coaching was very specific, and she knew me well enough to know which things I would be relieved to have him do, so Tony didn't have to think too much in order to get the job done. Because he was there and so supportive, I was able to go through the sadness and grief of losing my father without feeling burdened with other details and issues. It was unbelievable to be supported this way by both Terry and Tony. Ten years later, I'm still moved by the experience. I'm especially blown away that Tony cared so much about being there for me that he was willing to forgo his ego (that part of a man that won't stop and ask directions) and get help from Terry.

I also learned from this experience that there are times when even though I want to support Tony, I'm not always able. There are times when your spouse needs someone else to talk to or to get advice from besides you. Often they don't even see this. Several times I have seen Tony in a funk or confused and either I had too much going on myself to be there for him or I thought there was someone else who would be more suited and helpful to the situation. Tony was occasionally resistant to my suggestion of going elsewhere for "help," but every time he did it worked out so well that now he's always open to the idea.

Choose Your Friends Wisely

You can't go to just anyone for support, because not everyone supports your relationship. And that is the determining factor in asking for help. Unless the person (1) stands behind you, (2) admires and cares about your spouse, and (3) cares about the success of your marriage, don't go to them with your issues.

Your mother may love you unconditionally, but underneath, she may also think your husband is not good enough for you. If you go to her with complaints about him, she will readily agree with you. "I told you so. I always knew he was selfish and inconsiderate." Someone taking your side may temporarily feel good, but it won't help the matter.

You need someone who "knows" your husband and knows why you love him, so you can be reminded. "You're right, he was being a jerk, but you know he doesn't want to hurt you. He's probably defensive because he knows he's wrong. Tell him *you know* he didn't mean it, and it will probably start to clear up."

If someone doesn't support both of you, you can still be friends, just don't use that person when you need comfort or advice about your marriage.

The other group of people *not* to go to at these times are individuals who are newly divorced or veterans of multiple divorces. You already know what they are likely to think is the answer to your problems. Unless that's the answer you're certain you're looking for, stay away!

A while back, I ran into a friend's new wife. When I asked how things were going she said, "Pretty awful." I offered to meet with her alone or with the two of them. I was quite concerned by her response. "Oh, thanks, but Kent [a mutual friend] has been so wonderful and helpful. You know he's been married five times and really has learned a lot about what to do and not do." I tried to gently tell her that Kent's multiple failures were perhaps the wrong credentials, but she didn't agree. Three months later, she was divorced.

In addition to someone who is supportive of both of you, seek out successful role models. You'll get much more valuable advice from people who have made their relationships work through thick and thin than from those who have failed but "learned from their mistakes."

Don't Wait

Don't wait until the situation is critical before you seek help. People used to go to their parents or relatives for advice about even the smallest situations. Taking care of little annoyances in the early stages will prevent a major disturbance from erupting in the future. You will be amazed by the simplicity of the advice others offer and you hadn't thought of.

A week before I was about to leave on a horseback-riding vacation in Europe without Tony or the kids, I had a panic attack. "What if I got hurt, died, and never came back," I thought to myself. My will was in order, but still I was crazed. I talked it over with my friend Karen. She questioned me to find out specifically what was troubling me. It came down to a few things I worried Tony wouldn't do regarding the children if I wasn't there. For instance, I wanted to be sure they stayed in the same private school, that Jordan would continue his Hebrew lessons, and, if Tony should remarry, that the kids would remain his main priority.

Karen suggested I let Tony know what I wanted before I left and find out if he was willing to agree. I took her advice. Tony laughed when he heard my concerns, because everything I asked for he already agreed with. Still, he appreciated how I felt, and he used the occasion to let me know what he wanted should he die unexpectedly.

I was so grateful to Karen because she took the time to find out what was going on with me. The solution was obvious, except I was too emotional to even determine what the real problem was. She helped me clear the way to leave with my mind at ease so I was able to have a magnificent and stress-free vacation.

Find What's Best for You

Before problems become too great, seek professional counseling. There is still sometimes a stigma against therapy, as if by going to a counselor or therapist you are admitting weakness or defeat. Letting such feelings stop you from seeking assistance is as senseless as not going to an orthopedist to set a broken leg.

It's downright stupid to suffer unnecessarily when there are so many caring, proficient counselors available. Living with the hope that the problem will clear up and go away on its own is not a solution. Face it, you can't always handle it on your own.

What Can You Do for Others?

On the other side of the equation is your ability to support other people. Just as having a rash of divorces in your community tends to threaten the stability of your own marriage, having stronger, healthy relationships surround you will contribute to the health and strength of your own. Given this, it is only to your benefit to be a resource for other couples.

Don't be concerned over fears that you don't have the qualifications or enough experience. As I said earlier, just being an uninvolved third party can make a big difference. Just being someone who will listen without judgment and opinion, someone with whom your friends can talk their way through something, is an opportunity to practice giving without expecting anything in return.

Many times a couple doesn't know they are heading into trouble, and they need someone to point it out. A friend of mine was visiting from Los Angeles. As the two of us were "catching up" over a glass of wine, she said, "I have to tell you something I've observed. I may be way off base, and I don't want you to get mad, but I think you should hear this." I said go ahead, I could handle it.

She said she had noticed I wasn't speaking about Tony, or even to Tony, with much respect. She had observed me making demeaning comments and jokes, and quite a few sarcastic remarks. Having read my earlier book, she said it looked as if I had slid back into my old shtick.

Admittedly, I did not rejoice at hearing this news. At first I was defensive, denying what she said and then blaming Tony. But I quickly came around to seeing she was right. I was embarrassed and chagrined, yet, because she said something, I was able to "nip it in the bud" and make the necessary corrections in my behavior.

I recommend that with friends or family you really love and are committed to, do not wait until you're asked before you offer your assistance. It is often when we need help the most that we are least likely to ask for it. Especially with the people you care most about, take the chance and, by all means, risk being a little intrusive. If someone was drowning, would you wait until they cried for help before jumping into the water to save them?

I'm known for taking such risks, and in many instances, the initial reaction from my friends has been anger or even outrage. But in the end, in every case, the couple expressed gratitude that I cared enough to take the risk and talk to them. I am especially concerned when children are involved. If there's anything I can do to help protect the stability of a child's home, I've got to at least try. Though I don't particularly enjoy intruding into other people's private lives, I'm willing to take the chance of being disliked rather than answering to myself later if I feel I have let down someone I love.

This Isn't an Option

You may have gotten as far as you have without seeking support from others. But, I promise you, your relationship with your spouse will fall short of how extraordinary it could be unless you open up and allow your friends to enter your life on a more meaningful level. Even if you could do it on your own, it would be like reinventing the wheel—there is no glory in it and it is a tragic waste of time.

I'm the "relationship expert," the one who's writing this book, and even *I* know that when I'm in the midst of it with Tony, my expertise disappears. I need someone else to help me see what's going on. The statement, "a lawyer who represents himself in court has a fool for a client" fits equally well in relationships.

Exercises in Creating What You Want

A. What family or community resources could you use to support your relationship? Make a list of at least twenty classes or workshops you could take, books to read, groups or counseling available through your church or synagogue.

B. Who could you go to for advice and support regarding your marriage? Who do you trust and respect enough to help you when you need it? Make a list of at least ten people.

C. Use one of your one-hour conversation periods to discuss the two lists you have made with your spouse.

D. Are there friends or family you should make yourself available to in support of their relationships? Use another of your one-hour conversation periods to discuss this with your spouse.

Put Together
a Survival Kit

U$_p$ till now, this book has focused on not screwing up your relationship. This chapter is about how to take your relationship from ordinary to extraordinary, how to have a relationship that *keeps getting better,* growing more romantic, more passionate, more intimate.

Spend Time Together

Spend time together alone. Do something fun together at least once a week. If you wait until you have the time, it may never happen. So make the time, then guard it and protect it! If something has to be dropped from your schedule, make your date the absolute last thing that goes. And it's got to be time when you can talk to each other. While going to movies may be fun, to qualify as time alone you need to add having dinner or a drink before or after the film. Doing something together that's fun is absolutely the top priority. It is not a luxury. It is as vital to the well-being of your relationship as food is to your body.

Quite a few years ago Tony and I were on vacation with another couple. Each morning when we went over the schedule for the day, Terry would set aside time when she and her husband, Alan, would do something alone. I was envious of how romantic their relationship was and how much they wanted to be together. I thought Tony and I should be the ones acting this way; after all, we were the newlyweds; Terry and Alan had been married for ten years. So I started to schedule moonlight walks or late afternoon naps alone with Tony. 1 couldn't believe how easy it was.

This was the beginning of my education in romance. Like most couples newly in love, we had many wonderfully romantic moments, and I was determined to keep the passion alive in our marriage. But as unromantic as it sounds, I began to dissect these episodes in an attempt to discover what made them romantic. I found three common elements: surprise, planning or forethought, and action. The first two seem contradictory, but they're not.

Surprise can make even the smallest gesture seem enchanting and significant. Nothing is more romantic than receiving a love note under your pillow or a bouquet of flowers when you least expect it. Although it's wonderful to be given such expressions on birthdays or special occasions, the element of surprise adds something undeniable to the gift of being reminded of how much you are loved.

Unconsciously, I believed, as do most people, that romance "just happens." But even the most spontaneous moment involves planning. Think of the classic romantic moments in your life—sitting by a fire with soft music and a glass of wine, dinner by candlelight, or a love poem placed on your pillow. They all required forethought. Someone had to buy the candles and the wine and build the fire.

So whenever I hear the complaint that "he used to be so romantic," I tell the person to stop whining and do something about it. Quit waiting to "feel romantic." Take some action and the feelings will follow. "But we're too busy." You already know my answer to that complaint: You can't afford *not* to take the time. We're only talking about a few minutes, not hours or days. How long does it take to order flowers or sneak an "I miss you" note into your spouse's overnight bag before a business trip?

One fall I was traveling and presenting seminars almost every evening, so my schedule didn't allow much romantic time alone with Tony. It was a Tuesday, and I knew Tony and I wouldn't have another free evening together for a week. This was too long for me, so I sent a telegram to his office that said, "Meet me in front of the fireplace at 10:15 tonight. You make the fire, I'll supply the wine." It took absolutely no time at all for me to send the telegram or Tony to receive it, yet the romantic feelings began in that moment.

Have Some Fun

When you first start dating, you enjoy each other's company and have fun together. It's not just that you get along or you respect him or she has a great sense of humor. These things are important, but the main thing is you want to be together because it's enjoyable.

In my interviews with successful couples, without exception, they all say they had fun together from the very beginning. At least one of the two will have a great sense of humor, making it

easy for them to be playful with each other. I have found that
most people have this quality of playfulness in their relationship
in the beginning, but few couples manage to preserve it over the
years.

It's easy to get caught up in the business of living—working,
paying bills, doing chores, and managing the mundane details of
life. Living together can end up seeming so burdensome that
even picking a movie for a Saturday night date becomes another
item on the to-do list. Having "fun" with each other isn't even on
the agenda.

Most of this is just simple forgetfulness. We forget we can
have fun, and we forget our spouse is someone we want to have
fun with. We also forget that not only would going to the movies
be fun, but all the boring chores can become fun as well. It only
requires a slight change of attitude.

Our wedding is a good example. It was a beautiful Black and
White Ball that took place on a yacht that cruised around Puget
Sound during the celebration. Over the course of planning the
event, friends would ask, "You must have tons of work to do,
aren't you exhausted? stressed out? worried?" No. From the
start, Tony and I had a pact that we not only were going to have
a ball at "the ball," we were also going to enjoy each and every
part of the event, from ordering the wedding invitations to send-
ing thank-you notes. I didn't have to have this wedding, no one
was making me do it, and Tony would gladly have gone to Las
Vegas to avoid the entire hassle. So why have this elaborate event
if it wasn't going to be a kick?

We made each activity a "date." One of the most enjoyable of
these dates was the evening we spent writing up the invitation
list. As we sat at the dining room table with our address books
writing down names, it evolved into a riotous evening of telling
stories about our different relatives. Tony started by telling me

about his Aunt Nell. "The most amazing thing about Aunt Nell is the ash on the end of her cigarettes. As a child, while she talked on and on, all of us kids would stare at her in amazement, wondering how long the ash would get before it fell off or she noticed. It would grow inches long, bending over as we held our breaths and yet she would just go on yapping. Then, in the exact moment the ash fell, her free hand would magically drift over and catch it before it fell to the floor. She would never bat an eye or stop talking, but we would gasp and squirm in amazement. Our parents could never figure out what we found so fascinating about Aunt Nell."

This led to stories and jokes about my relatives and friends, and soon we were switching back and forth, one-upping each other and howling. Not only did our lists get done, but it gave us a preview of who we would meet at the wedding and greater insight into each other and the families we were marrying into. I can't tell you the disappointment I felt when I heard Aunt Nell would not be able to attend the wedding.

Whenever Tony and I are about to go into a potentially stressful, boring, or unpleasant situation, we look for a way to make it more enjoyable. The first couple of Thanksgivings with Tony's parents we waited hours for dinner feeling hungry and bored. So I began bringing plenty of scrumptious appetizers to tide us over until the main "feast." Also, Tony and I decided to come up with an activity involving the entire family. One year, we interviewed Tony's parents about their parents and their childhoods. The next year everyone, including the children, had to read a poem, sing a song, play an instrument, or present a skit.

Waiting in airports, Tony and I make up stories about people who pass by or we might compare our candidates for best and worst dressed. On long drives we talk about what we would do and in what order if we won the lottery. It's fun to fantasize and to compare what we say we would do now with the last time we had the discussion or how what we want has changed over the last ten years. We talk about anything and everything, from what jobs we would like to have to what countries we would like to visit. And, of course, the kids give us hours of talking pleasure, from discussing what they said and did that day to what we think they will be like when they are older.

Do something you've never done before—go bowling or hiking under a full moon, spend an evening baking cookies together or reading a book out loud to each other. If the normal evening is spent watching television together, break the pattern. Stop waiting for gaiety and romance to spontaneously appear and *do* something to bring these experiences back into your life and marriage.

Vacations

Vacations for just the two of you are a must. Isn't this great news? In order to have a healthy, vibrant, extraordinary relationship, you *have* to take vacations together. You need pleasurable, relaxing time together where you can be romantic, intimate, playful, where you can become best friends all over again and deepen the love you have for each other.

Vacations take planning. And planning and scheduling these vacations needs to be given a high priority. Otherwise, they don't seem to happen, or you find yourselves using your time off hanging around the house. "Home alone" does not produce the same result for your relationship as a cabin in the mountains or a bed and breakfast in the country.

Many people find the planning part troublesome or boring, while others find the preparation almost as much fun as the

actual vacation. Find out which of you is best at this initial
phase and let them take the lead. And there is lots to do. You
need to know when you're taking the time off, where you want to
go, and how much it will cost. Then you need to save or find the
money from one of your accounts; arrange for the care of the
children, pets, and plants; and make all the necessary travel
arrangements or make sure the camping gear is in order.

I love vacations. And I've had lots of practice, yet even with
all of my experience, it's still not easy. Because I want to take
vacations so frequently, it seems we never have enough money in
our vacation account. So I'm always researching bargains and
depending on frequent flyer miles to travel. I've been known to
spend hours at a time on the phone with the airlines trying to
figure out when I can use our miles, what flights we have to take
in order to reach our destination for the least possible cost, and
how to book around the various "black-out" periods.

Then I have to deal with Tony! Although he's the greatest and
most fun person once we get to where we're going, he's terrible
in the planning and preparation stages. His point of view is that
we can't afford to be going on the trip, whether we are talking
about spending a night in a hotel in town or a week in Paris. And
Tony "can't leave work." We will plan our vacation perhaps three
months in advance, then as we get close to the departure date,
Tony always comes home with a critical situation at his job that
"absolutely requires" him to be there. It is as predictable as the
sunrise that three weeks before our departure Tony will ask
me to find out how much we will lose in cancellation fees if we
don't go.

At this juncture I would usually lose my cool. Vacations to me
are akin to Christmas for a child, and everyone knows how dev-
astating it would be to cancel Christmas. I tried everything,
including crying, being "understanding," volunteering to help

him with some of his backlog, but many times I just got mad. "You always do this!" I would yell. To which he would reply, "I told you not to plan this trip until things were cleared at the office," and so on, back and forth. Eventually, I would reluctantly agree we could go some other time. Then, after going through this predictable cycle of events, a miracle would happen, everything would turn out, and we always ended up going on vacation. I'm learning though. Now, when Tony starts talking about how he won't be able to leave work, my response is, "That's awful, darling, I'm really going to miss you." Tony hasn't missed a vacation yet.

So even for me, the "master" at planning vacations, it isn't easy to make these trips work out. It's particularly difficult to go away without our children. We both love being with our kids, especially on vacations. We have yet to *want* to leave them. Fortunately, we know enough to do it, and it always turns out to be wonderful. Even one night away will do the trick and get us back together as a couple.

Our former baby-sitter is now married and has two children of her own. Recently, after returning from a long weekend with her husband, she said to me, "Now I know what you meant when you would come home from a weekend with Tony and say you had fallen in love with your husband again. It's not that Ron and I haven't been getting along, but we've been so involved with the kids we'd forgotten who we were as a couple."

Many people keep putting off vacations, and for valid reasons. "We don't have the money," or "We don't have the time," or "We don't have anyone who can stay with the kids," and so on. If you give in to your reasons, the vacation probably will never happen. You are doing it backwards. First, plan the vacation, then learn how much money and time and help is needed so you can incorporate what you need into the entire process.

Even if all you can do is take a long weekend together, do it. Go to the ocean or the mountains, or camping somewhere near your home. It doesn't have to cost much money, nor does it need to be an extended trip. Just make sure it's the two of you and plan it so that it's romantic. Or, if you are going with other people, carve out time for the two of you to be alone and guard this time as precious. You may not be used to spending so much time alone—it may even be uncomfortable at first—but that is why it is so necessary. Use the time to find out new things about each other and have the conversations you never seem to have at home. This is a time to share your dreams, your concerns, your wounds, and your fantasies.

Goals

In addition to financial and career goals, I strongly recommend you make goals for every other area of your life at least once a year.

Goal-setting is a key ingredient in achieving success. Looking ahead allows you to see abilities and opportunities that otherwise would go unnoticed. But the most significant benefit of goal-setting is the boost it gives your mental and physical health and well-being. People want and need to grow, and setting goals introduces a kind of boldness into our thinking and actions. The way to stay young is to think young, and that means continuing to dream.

What I suggest you do is take three pieces of paper and label them as follows:

1. What do I want to *be* this year?
2. What do I want to *do* this year?
3. What do I want to *have* this year?

Then write down what comes to mind. Don't let reality, practicality, or your bank account edit what you write. The only qualification needed to put something on your list is whether or not you want it, not whether you can or should have it.

I also recommend you set specific goals for your relationship. In a section at the bottom of each of these pages (or on additional pages) print the heading "Relationship Goals." Then, under this heading, write the *"be"* goals for your relationship. For example, you might have a goal to be romantic, or be attentive, or be affectionate. For *"do"* goals, you may have a goal to go to Hawaii, take dance lessons, or go out on a "date" at least once a week. *"Haves"* could include getting a new house, some romantic CDs, or new bedroom linens. It only takes an hour or so to do this process, and a one-hour-a-year investment for some pretty amazing results is not asking a great deal.

Tony and I have a tradition on New Year's Eve. We each have the assignment of preparing our goals for the coming year beforehand. At dinner, we review our new goals as well as the goals we wrote the previous year. First we look at the year just ending, checking off everything that was achieved and adding any major accomplishments that were not on the list for the year. We talk about the highlights as well as the low points of the year. We discuss what we are grateful for, and we discuss our disappointments. Often this is a time we acknowledge each other, apologize, and forgive.

We then share our new goals with each other. This conversation often inspires new personal goals as well as new goals for the relationship. As we go over the list for the coming year, we always look for those activities we can do together and pick the ones we want to take on that year with particular enthusiasm. Also, this is the time we set our vacation goals, including when and where we would like to go.

Before we began doing this, New Year's Eve was always anti-climactic. Even the great parties weren't significant enough and the romantic dinners alone didn't do it either. Now that we have created this process as our own special tradition, New Year's Eve is very intimate, extremely romantic, and much more meaningful. It is so much fun and has worked so well, we have extended the tradition to creating goals with our children on New Year's Day.

Expand Your Horizons

One sure way to combat "growing apart" is to grow together.

There are a million possibilities that will further this end. Start with the things you've always wanted to do but haven't and compare your lists to see if you can agree on something you can do together. You may have always wanted to take fly-fishing lessons, and he has wanted to take a course on the Bible or a series of lectures on English literature. If neither is willing to do the other's choice, keep working on it until you reach some consensus.

You don't have to have a burning desire to try something new. The point is to be *open* to new ideas and to change. Initially, you may not be thrilled with whatever you choose, but once you get engaged you may discover an interest that ends up becoming a passion. One year Tony and I enrolled in a music appreciation class. By the third class we were both so totally bored we skipped out at the break never to return. To replace the music class, we started studying religion, which completely captivated both of us and brought an element of spirituality into our lives that I now can't imagine living without.

Every year Tony and I also participate in some kind of personal growth workshop, class, or seminar. These programs are not necessarily couples courses, but we find doing them together is nurturing and healthy for us as a couple.

Here are some ideas and areas to look into for your ongoing growth:

> Take a class together:
> Cooking
> Language
> Music
> Dancing
> Religion
> Philosophy
> Psychology
> Carpentry
> Art
> Computers
>
> Take on a new sport or further develop one you already know:
> Skiing
> Fishing
> Golf
> Bowling
> Horseback riding
> Hiking
>
> Volunteer together:
> At a museum
> For a political candidate
> For a charity
> At a hospital, hospice, or shelter

Work on benefits or fund-raising for a cause you
support
At your children's school

Attend:
Sporting events
The theater, opera, or symphony
Rock concerts
Lectures
Seminars and workshops

You get the point. Try new things, and try them together. There is no such thing as coasting in life. You're either expanding and growing, or you are contracting. Support each other in growing and learning new things, not just as a couple but as individuals as well. Remember, nothing is more attractive than a partner who is awake, alive, and passionate about life.

Anniversaries

Any excuse to celebrate, eat cake, and get presents gets my full endorsement. I'm also in favor of every opportunity to celebrate, cherish, and empower your marriage. Anniversaries are a perfect occasion to nurture your relationship by expressing your love and appreciation.

My advice is to make it a big deal, even if you are not feeling particularly good about the marriage at the time or you are not feeling especially loving toward your spouse. Especially when you are not feeling loving is the time you should make a big hoopla. Remember what I said in Chapter 3 about how you can turn your relationship around by speaking about it differently? This could be your chance to try out my theory.

Your anniversary should be given as much importance and fanfare as you would your child's birthday. After all, it *is* the birthday of your marriage. Don't settle for the usual dinner and some token gifts. Do something that will make it memorable and be a tribute to you as a couple. One couple I know uses their anniversary to do their goal-setting. Another couple travels to a different romantic spot for their yearly honeymoon, even booking the honeymoon suite if there is one.

Tony and I try to do something different every year. Usually a couple of weeks before, we plan what we want to do and then create assignments for ourselves. One year we each wrote a story about the history of our marriage. Another year, it was a poem. Another time, we each created a photographic collage or album. On our fifth anniversary, we both came prepared with the top five moments of the year for us as a couple. The last couple of years we've taken advantage of the mountains of New Mexico and hiked different peaks. Then, at the summit we discuss our assignment over wine and cheese.

Review and Renew Those Vows

Anniversaries are an excellent time for renewing your marriage vows. Doing this every year might be too much, but I do recommend you do it every five years and, at the very least, at the end of each decade together.

Renewing your vows is an opportunity to look at your marriage and to renew it with empowering and appropriate promises. These promises can be the same as your original vows, but are likely to be more personal, more tailored to the two of you, and probably a lot more meaningful.

We went to a tenth anniversary celebration of friends who

renewed their vows in front of a group of people, many of whom had been at the wedding. This renewal of the original vows was a far more moving and inspiring occasion. In a time of so much divorce, it was encouraging and uplifting to celebrate a passionate and loving marriage that has lasted.

Exercises in Creating What You Want

A. Schedule your next vacation for just the two of you. Set a date, decide where you are going, determine the budget, and take the necessary actions to make it happen.

B. Do something really romantic with or for your spouse this week.

C. Do something incredibly fun with your spouse this week.

D. Schedule time and do a goal-setting session with your spouse.

E. In the goal-setting session, look at and choose a project, class, or interest in which the two of you will participate together.

F. Write down the vows you would like to make for your marriage and renew these vows with each other.

How Not to Fail

A healthy relationship is one that continues to get better, more loving, closer, and more and more nurturing to each partner. This book has presented two radical ideas or paths to achieving this. One is a program or path of creativity, of designing ways to keep bringing life to your life together. It includes the various exercises in creating what you want, such as the daily one-hour talks, having sex frequently, spending time alone, expressing appreciation for one another, making sure you have time together for fun, romance, and exciting vacations. The other path deals with what to do when you are having problems. Often, simply reigniting the spark of creativity when things get stale will reenliven you both and head off more difficult problems. Each chapter, however, also gives specific advice for working out problems. And always, always, look to others you trust for wisdom, help, and support. You never have to totally rely on your own resources to come up with all the answers.

Where you do have to look is to yourself alone in your personal commitment and determination to make your relationship work. *You* are the one who will make or break your marriage, and *you* are the one who is ultimately in control.

There is a story, perhaps apocryphal, about Winston Churchill near the end of his life. He was to speak to the assembled student body at Cambridge University. After a lengthy introduction extolling his long career in politics, his great defeats and greater victories, and his stature as one of the giant figures of the century, the man himself, obviously infirm, slowly rose from his chair. Even more slowly, he made his way to the podium. Finally, in that wonderful voice that had sustained the British people through the darkest days of World War II, he spoke. "Never, never, never, never, never, never, never give up," he said. Then he sat down.

I've worked with enough couples in enough circumstances to know you can have not just a relationship that survives the ups and downs but the very one you have always dreamed of having. And you can have it with the spouse you already have. If *you* take on the project of having your marriage be extraordinary, then you *will* succeed.

The only way you can fail is if you give up. Never give up!